FIRES

FIRES

ESSAYS

POEMS

STORIES

RAYMOND CARVER

VINTAGE BOOKS
A DIVISION OF RANDOM HOUSE
NEW YORK

First Vintage Books Edition, March 1984

Special thanks to George Hitchcock for permission to reprint several poems from *Winter
Insomnia*, a Kayak Press book. Some of the poems were published in *At Night the Salmon
Move*, Capra Press. Many of the poems first appeared, some in different versions, in *Akros
Review, Antioch Review, Beloit Poetry Journal, Carolina Quarterly, Chelsea, Colorado
Quarterly, Crazy Horse, Cutbank, December, Discourse, Esquire, Harper's, Ironwood,
Kayak, Midwest Quarterly Review, Mississippi Review, Missouri Review, New England
Review, Ploughshares, Poetry Now, Prairie Schooner, Prism International, Quarry, Quarterly
West, Tendril, Transatlantic Review, West Coast Review, Western Humanities Review.*

"Distress Sale" (1981) was published as a Broadside by Lord John Press. "The Baker" and
"Louise" (1982) were published in limited edition by Scarab Press, Salisbury, Maryland.

Thanks are also due the editors of these anthologies: *The Poet's Choice,
New Voices in American Poetry, Out of This World, The Brand-X Anthology of Poetry,*
and *The Poem As Process.*

"On Writing" first appeared in the New York Times Book Review as "A Storyteller's
Notebook," February 15, 1981. © The New York Times Company. Used by permission.
"On Writing" also appeared in *Short Short Stories.* © 1982 by Holt, Rinehart
and Winston of Canada, Ltd.

"Fires" © *Antaeus*, No. 47, Autumn 1982. Used by permission. The essay also appeared,
in a somewhat different form, in *Syracuse Scholar* 3, No. 2; and it was included in *In Praise
of What Persists.* © 1983, Harper and Row, Inc. Grateful acknowledgement to the
editors for permission to reprint.

The author also thanks the editors of the magazines where the short stories first appeared,
in some cases in slightly altered form: *American Poetry Review, Chariton Review,
Indiana Review, Iowa Review, New England Review, Playgirl, TriQuarterly,* and *Western
Humanities Review.* Thanks as well to James D. Houston, editor, *West Coast Fiction*
(Bantam Books), and Bill Henderson, editor, *The Pushcart Prize: Best of the Small Presses.*

"The Pheasant" was first published in limited edition by Metacom Press in September 1982.

"So Much Water So Close to Home," "The Lie," "Distance," "The Cabin" (original title
"Pastoral") were included in *Furious Seasons*, Capra Press, 1977.

"So Much Water So Close to Home," "Where Is Everyone?" and "Distance"
("Everything Stuck to Him") appeared, in different form, in *What We Talk About When
We Talk About Love.* Alfred A. Knopf, Inc. © 1981 by Raymond Carver.

Grateful acknowledgment is made to Mona Simpson and Lewis Buzbee for permission
to reprint the interview with Raymond Carver, by Mona Simpson and Lewis Buzbee.
Originally published in *The Paris Review.*

Library of Congress Cataloging in Publication Data
Carver, Raymond.
Fires.
I. Title.
[PS3553.A7894F5 1984]   813'.54   83-40305
ISBN 0-394-72299-X (pbk.)

For Tess

And isn't the past inevitable,
now that we call the little
we remember of it "the past"?

WILLIAM MATTHEWS, "Flood"

CONTENTS

STORIES

THE PARIS REVIEW INTERVIEW

AFTERWORD

ESSAYS

ON WRITING

Back in the mid-1960s, I found I was having trouble concentrating my attention on long narrative fiction. For a time I experienced difficulty in trying to read it as well as in attempting to write it. My attention span had gone out on me; I no longer had the patience to try to write novels. It's an involved story, too tedious to talk about here. But I know it has much to do now with why I write poems and short stories. Get in, get out. Don't linger. Go on. It could be that I lost any great ambitions at about the same time, in my late twenties. If I did, I think it was good it happened. Ambition and a little luck are good things for a writer to have going for him. Too much ambition and bad luck, or no luck at all, can be killing. There has to be talent.

Some writers have a bunch of talent; I don't know any writers who are without it. But a unique and exact way of looking at things, and finding the right context for expressing that way of looking, that's something else. *The World According to Garp* is, of course, the marvelous world according to John Irving. There is another world according to Flannery O'Connor, and others according to William Faulkner and Ernest Hemingway. There are worlds according to Cheever, Updike, Singer, Stanley Elkin, Ann Beattie, Cynthia Ozick, Donald Barthelme, Mary Robison, William Kittredge, Barry Hannah, Ursula K. LeGuin. Every great or even every very good writer makes the world over according to his own specifications.

It's akin to style, what I'm talking about, but it isn't style alone. It is the writer's particular and unmistakable signature on everything he writes. It is his world and no other. This is one of the things that distinguishes one writer from another. Not talent. There's plenty of that around. But a writer who has some special way of looking at things and who gives artistic expression to that way of looking: that writer may be around for a time.

Isak Dinesen said that she wrote a little every day, without hope and without despair. Someday I'll put that on a three-by-five card and tape it to the wall beside my desk. I have some three-by-five cards on the wall now. "Fundamental accuracy of statement is the ONE sole morality of writing." Ezra Pound. It is not everything by ANY means, but if a writer has "fundamental accuracy of statement" going for him, he's at least on the right track.

I have a three-by-five up there with this fragment of a sentence from a story by Chekov: "...and suddenly everything became clear to him." I find these words filled with wonder and possibility. I love their simple clarity, and the hint of revelation that's implied. There is mystery, too. What has been unclear before? Why is it just now becoming clear? What's happened? Most of all—what now? There are consequences as a result of such sudden awakenings. I feel a sharp sense of relief—and anticipation.

I overheard the writer Geoffrey Wolff say "No cheap tricks" to a group of writing students. That should go on a three-by-five card. I'd amend it a little to "No tricks." Period. I hate tricks. At the first sign of a trick or a gimmick in a piece of fiction, a cheap trick or even an elaborate trick, I tend to look for cover. Tricks are ultimately boring, and I get bored easily, which may go along with my not having much of an attention span. But extremely clever chi-chi writing, or just plain tomfoolery writing, puts me to sleep. Writers don't need tricks or gimmicks or even necessarily need to be the smartest fellows on the block. At the risk of appearing foolish, a writer sometimes needs to be able to just stand and gape at this or that thing—a sunset or an old shoe—in absolute and simple amazement.

Some months back, in the *New York Times Book Review*, John Barth said that ten years ago most of the students in his fiction writing seminar were interested in "formal innovation," and this no longer seems to be the case. He's a little worried that writers are going to start writing mom and pop novels in the 1980s. He worries that experimentation may be on the way out, along with liberalism. I get a little nervous if I find myself within earshot of somber discussions about "formal innovation" in fiction writing. Too often "experimentation" is a license to be careless, silly or imitative in the writing. Even worse, a license to try to brutalize or alienate the reader. Too often such writing gives us no news of the world, or else describes a desert landscape and that's all—a few dunes and lizards here and there, but no people; a place uninhabited by anything recognizably human, a place of interest only to a few scientific specialists.

It should be noted that real experiment in fiction is original, hard-earned and cause for rejoicing. But someone else's way of looking at things—Barthelme's, for instance—should not be chased after by other writers. It won't work. There is only one Barthelme, and for another writer to try to appropriate Barthelme's peculiar sensibility or *mise en scene* under the rubric of innovation is for that writer to mess around with chaos and disaster and, worse, self-deception. The real experimenters have to Make It New, as Pound urged, and in the process have to find things out for themselves. But if writers haven't taken leave of their senses, they also want to stay in touch with us, they want to carry news from their world to ours.

It's possible, in a poem or a short story, to write about commonplace things and objects using commonplace but precise language, and to endow those things—a chair, a window curtain, a fork, a stone, a woman's earring—with immense, even startling power. It is possible to write a line of seemingly innocuous dialogue and have it send a chill along the reader's spine—the source of artistic delight, as Nabokov would have it. That's the kind of writing that most interests me. I hate sloppy or haphazard writing whether it flies under the banner of experimentation or else is just clumsily rendered realism. In Isaac Babel's wonderful short story, "Guy de Maupassant," the narrator has this to say about the writing of fiction: "No iron can pierce the heart with such force as a period put just at the right place." This too ought to go on a three-by-five.

Evan Connell said once that he knew he was finished with a short story when he found himself going through it and taking out commas and then going through the story again and putting commas back in the same places. I like that way of working on something. I respect that kind of care for what is being done. That's all we have, finally, the words, and they had better be the right ones, with the punctuation in the right places so that they can best say what they are meant to say. If the words are heavy with the writer's own unbridled emotions, or if they are imprecise and inaccurate for some other reason—if the words are in any way blurred—the reader's eyes will slide right over them and nothing will be achieved. The reader's own artistic sense will simply not be engaged. Henry James called this sort of hapless writing "weak specification."

I have friends who've told me they had to hurry a book because they needed the money, their editor or their wife was leaning on them or leaving them—something, some apology for the writing not being very good. "It would have been better if I'd taken the time." I was dumbfounded when I heard a novelist friend say this. I still am, if I think about it, which I don't. It's none of my business. But if the writing can't be made as good as it is within us to make it, then why do it? In the end, the satisfaction of having done our best, and the proof of that labor, is the one thing we can take into the grave. I wanted to say to my friend, for heaven's sake go do something else. There have to be easier and maybe more honest ways to try and earn a living. Or else just do it to the best of your abilities, your talents, and then don't justify or make excuses. Don't complain, don't explain.

In an essay called, simply enough, "Writing Short Stories," Flannery O'Connor talks about writing as an act of discovery. O'Connor says she most often did not know where she was going when she sat down to work on a short story. She says she doubts that many writers know where they are going when they begin something. She uses "Good Country People" as an example of how she put together a short story whose ending she could not even guess at until she was nearly there:

> When I started writing that story, I didn't know there was going to be a Ph.D. with a wooden leg in it. I merely found myself one morning writing a description of two women I knew something about, and before I realized it, I had equipped one of them with a daughter with a wooden leg. I brought in the Bible salesman, but I had no idea what I was going to do

with him. I didn't know he was going to steal that wooden leg
until ten or twelve lines before he did it, but when I found out
that this was what was going to happen, I realized it was inevitable.

When I read this some years ago it came as a shock that she, or
anyone for that matter, wrote stories in this fashion. I thought this
was my uncomfortable secret, and I was a little uneasy with it. For
sure I thought this way of working on a short story somehow
revealed my own shortcomings. I remember being tremendously
heartened by reading what she had to say on the subject.

I once sat down to write what turned out to be a pretty good
story, though only the first sentence of the story had offered itself
to me when I began it. For several days I'd been going around with
this sentence in my head: "He was running the vacuum cleaner
when the telephone rang." I knew a story was there and that it
wanted telling. I felt it in my bones, that a story belonged with that
beginning, if I could just have the time to write it. I found the time,
an entire day—twelve, fifteen hours even—if I wanted to make use
of it. I did, and I sat down in the morning and wrote the first
sentence, and other sentences promptly began to attach themselves. I made the story just as I'd make a poem; one line and then
the next, and the next. Pretty soon I could see a story, and I knew it
was my story, the one I'd been wanting to write.

I like it when there is some feeling of threat or sense of menace
in short stories. I think a little menace is fine to have in a story.
For one thing, it's good for the circulation. There has to be tension,
a sense that something is imminent, that certain things are in
relentless motion, or else, most often, there simply won't be a
story. What creates tension in a piece of fiction is partly the way
the concrete words are linked together to make up the visible
action of the story. But it's also the things that are left out, that are
implied, the landscape just under the smooth (but sometimes
broken and unsettled) surface of things.

V.S. Pritchett's definition of a short story is "something glimpsed
from the corner of the eye, in passing." Notice the "glimpse" part of
this. First the glimpse. Then the glimpse given life, turned into
something that illuminates the moment and may, if we're lucky—
that word again—have even further-ranging consequences and

meaning. The short story writer's task is to invest the glimpse with all that is in his power. He'll bring his intelligence and literary skill to bear (his talent), his sense of proportion and sense of the fitness of things: of how things out there really are and how he sees those things—like no one else sees them. And this is done through the use of clear and specific langage, language used so as to bring to life the details that will light up the story for the reader. For the details to be concrete and convey meaning, the language must be accurate and precisely given. The words can be so precise they may even sound flat, but they can still carry; if used right, they can hit all the notes.

FIRES

Influences are forces—circumstances, personalities, irresistible as the tide. I can't talk about books or writers who might have influenced me. That kind of influence, literary influence, is hard for me to pin down with any kind of certainty. It would be as inaccurate for me to say I've been influenced by everything I've read as for me to say I don't think I've been influenced by any writers. For instance, I've long been a fan of Ernest Hemingway's novels and short stories. Yet I think Lawrence Durrell's work is singular and unsurpassed in the language. Of course, I don't write like Durrell. He's certainly no "influence." On occasion it's been said that my writing is "like" Hemingway's writing. But I can't say his writing influenced mine. Hemingway is one of the many writers whose work, like Durrell's, I first read and admired when I was in my twenties.

So I don't know about literary influences. But I do have some notions about other kinds of influences. The influences I know something about have pressed on me in ways that were often mysterious at first glance, sometimes stopping just short of the miraculous. But these influences have become clear to me as my work has progressed. These influences were (and they still are) relentless. These were the influences that sent me in this direction, onto this spit of land instead of some other—that one over there on the far side of the lake, for example. But if the main influence on my life and writing has been a negative one, oppressive and often malevolent, as I believe is the case, what am I to make of this?

Let me begin by saying that I'm writing this at a place called Yaddo, which is just outside of Saratoga Springs, New York. It's afternoon, Sunday, early August. Every so often, every twenty-five minutes or so, I can hear upwards of thirty thousand voices joined in a great outcry. This wonderful clamor comes from the Saratoga race

19

course. A famous meet is in progress. I'm writing, but every twenty-five minutes I can hear the announcer's voice coming over the loudspeaker as he calls the positions of the horses. The roar of the crowd increases. It bursts over the trees, a great and truly thrilling sound, rising until the horses have crossed the finish line. When it's over, I feel spent, as if I too had participated. I can imagine holding pari-mutuel tickets on one of the horses who finished in the money, or even a horse who came close. If it's a photo finish at the wire, I can expect to hear another outburst a minute or two later, after the film has been developed and the official results posted.

For several days now, ever since arriving here and upon first hearing the announcer's voice over the loudspeaker, and the excited roar from the crowd, I've been writing a short story set in El Paso, a city where I lived for a while some time ago. The story has to do with some people who go to a horse race at a track outside of El Paso. I don't want to say the story has been waiting to be written. It hasn't, and it would make it sound like something else to say that. But I needed something, in the case of this particular story, to push it out into the open. Then after I arrived here at Yaddo and first heard the crowd, and the announcer's voice over the loudspeaker, certain things came back to me from that other life in El Paso and suggested the story. I remembered that track I went to down there and some things that took place, that might have taken place, that *will* take place—in my story anyway—two thousand miles away from here.

So my story is under way, and there is that aspect of "influences." Of course, every writer is subject to this kind of influence. This is the most common kind of influence—*this* suggests that, *that* suggests something else. It's the kind of influence that is as common to us, and as natural, as rain water.

But before I go on to what I want to talk about, let me give one more example of influence akin to the first. Not so long ago in Syracuse, where I live, I was in the middle of writing a short story when my telephone rang. I answered it. On the other end of the line was the voice of a man who was obviously a black man, someone asking for a party named Nelson. It was a wrong number and I said so and hung up. I went back to my short story. But pretty soon I found myself writing a black character into my story, a somewhat sinister character whose name was Nelson. At that moment the story took a different turn. But happily it was, I see now, and somehow knew at the time, the right turn for the story. When I began to write that story, I could not have prepared for or predicted the necessity for the presence of Nelson in the story. But now, the story finished and about to appear in a national magazine, I see it is right and appropriate and, I believe, aesthetically correct, that Nelson be there, and be there with his sinister aspect. Also right for me is that this character found his way into my story with a coincidental rightness I had the good sense to trust.

I have a poor memory. By this I mean that much that has happened in my life I've forgotten—a blessing for sure—but I have these large periods of time I simply can't account for or bring back, towns and cities I've lived in, names of people, the people themselves. Large blanks. But I can remember some things. Little things —somebody saying something in a particular way; somebody's wild, or low, nervous laughter; a landscape; an expression of sadness or bewilderment on somebody's face; and I can remember some dramatic things—somebody picking up a knife and turning to me in anger; or else hearing my own voice threaten somebody else. Seeing somebody break down a door, or else fall down a flight of stairs. Some of those more dramatic kinds of memories I can recall when it's necessary. But I don't have the kind of memory that can bring entire conversations back to the present, complete with all the gestures and nuances of real speech; nor can I recall the furnishings of any room I've ever spent time in, not to mention my inability to remember the furnishings of an entire household. Or even very many specific things about a race track—except, let's see, a grandstand, betting windows, closed-circuit TV screens, masses of people. Hubbub. I make up the conversations in my stories. I put the furnishings and the physical things surrounding the people into the stories as I need those things. Perhaps this is why it's sometimes been said that my stories are unadorned, stripped down, even "minimalist." But maybe it's nothing more than a working marriage of necessity and convenience that has brought me to writing the kind of stories I do in the way that I do.

None of my stories really *happened*, of course—I'm not writing autobiography—but most of them bear a resemblance, however faint, to certain life occurrences or situations. But when I try to recall the physical surroundings or furnishings bearing on a story situation (what kind of flowers, if any, were present? Did they give off any odor? etc.), I'm often at a total loss. So I have to make it up as I go along—what the people in the story say to each other, as well as what they do then, after thus and so was said, and what happens to them next. I make up what they say to each other, though there may be, in the dialogue, some actual phrase, or sentence or two, that I once heard given in a particular context at some time or other. That sentence may even have been my starting point for the story.

When Henry Miller was in his forties and was writing *Tropic of Cancer*, a book, incidentally, that I like very much, he talks about trying to write in this borrowed room, where at any minute he may have to stop writing because the chair he is sitting on may be taken out from under him. Until fairly recently, this state of affairs persisted in my own life. For as long as I can remember, since I was a teen-ager, the imminent removal of the chair from under me was a constant concern. For years and years my wife and I met ourselves coming and going as we tried to keep a roof over our heads and put bread and milk on the table. We had no money, no visible, that is to say, marketable skills—nothing that we could do toward earning anything better than a get-by living. And we had no education, though we each wanted one very badly. Education, we believed, would open doors for us, help us get jobs so that we could make the kind of life we wanted for ourselves and our children. We had great dreams, my wife and I. We thought we could bow our necks, work very hard, and do all that we had set our hearts to do. But we were mistaken.

I have to say that the greatest single influence on my life, and on my writing, directly and indirectly, has been my two children. They were born before I was twenty, and from beginning to end of our habitation under the same roof—some nineteen years in all— there wasn't any area of my life where their heavy and often baleful influence didn't reach.

In one of her essays Flannery O'Connor says that not much needs to happen in a writer's life after the writer is twenty years old. Plenty of the stuff that makes fiction has already happened to

the writer before that time. More than enough, she says. Enough
things to last the writer the rest of his creative life. This is not true
for me. Most of what now strikes me as story "material" presented
itself to me after I was twenty. I really don't remember much about
my life before I became a parent. I really don't feel that anything
happened in my life until I was twenty and married and had the
kids. Then things started to happen.

In the mid 1960s I was in a busy laundromat in Iowa City trying to
do five or six loads of clothes, kids' clothes, for the most part, but
some of our own clothing, of course, my wife's and mine. My wife
was working as a waitress for the University Athletic Club that
Saturday afternoon. I was doing chores and being responsible for
the kids. They were with some other kids that afternoon, a birthday party maybe. Something. But right then I was doing the
laundry. I'd already had sharp words with an old harridan over the
number of washers I'd had to use. Now I was waiting for the next
round with her, or someone else like her. I was nervously keeping
an eye on the dryers that were in operation in the crowded laundromat. When and if one of the dryers ever stopped, I planned to rush
over to it with my shopping basket of damp clothes. Understand,
I'd been hanging around in the laundromat for thirty minutes or so
with this basketful of clothes, waiting my chance. I'd already
missed out on a couple of dryers—somebody'd gotten there first. I
was getting frantic. As I say, I'm not sure where our kids were that
afternoon. Maybe I had to pick them up from someplace, and it
was getting late, and that contributed to my state of mind. I did
know that even if I could get my clothes into a dryer it would still
be another hour or more before the clothes would dry, and I could
sack them up and go home with them, back to our apartment in
married-student housing. Finally a dryer came to a stop. And I was
right there when it did. The clothes inside quit tumbling and lay
still. In thirty seconds or so, if no one showed up to claim them, I
planned to get rid of the clothes and replace them with my own.
That's the law of the laundromat. But at that minute a woman
came over to the dryer and opened the door. I stood there waiting.
This woman put her hand into the machine and took hold of some
items of clothing. But they weren't dry enough, she decided. She
closed the door and put two more dimes into the machine. In a

daze I moved away with my shopping cart and went back to waiting. But I remember thinking at that moment, amid the feelings of helpless frustration that had me close to tears, that nothing—and, brother, I mean nothing—that ever happened to me on this earth could come anywhere close, could possibly be as important to me, could make as much difference, as the fact that I had two children. And that I would always have them and always find myself in this position of unrelieved responsibility and permanent distraction.

I'm talking about real *influence* now. I'm talking about the moon and the tide. But like that it came to me. Like a sharp breeze when the window is thrown open. Up to that point in my life I'd gone along thinking, what exactly, I don't know, but that things would work out somehow—that everything in my life I'd hoped for or wanted to do, was possible. But at that moment, in the laundromat, I realized that this simply was not true. I realized—what had I been thinking before?—that my life was a small-change thing for the most part, chaotic, and without much light showing through. At that moment I felt—I knew—that the life I was in was vastly different from the lives of the writers I most admired. I understood writers to be people who didn't spend their Saturdays at the laundromat and every waking hour subject to the needs and caprices of their children. Sure, sure, there've been plenty of writers who have had far more serious impediments to their work, including imprisonment, blindness, the threat of torture or of death in one form or another. But knowing this was no consolation. At that moment—I swear all of this took place there in the laundromat—I could see nothing ahead but years more of this kind of responsibility and perplexity. Things would change some, but they were never really going to get better. I understood this, but could I live with it? At that moment I saw accommodations would have to be made. The sights would have to be lowered. I'd had, I realized later, an insight. But so what? What are insights? They don't help any. They just make things harder.

For years my wife and I had held to a belief that if we worked hard and tried to do the right things, the right things would happen. It's not such a bad thing to try and build a life on. Hard work, goals, good intentions, loyalty, we believed these were virtues and would someday be rewarded. We dreamt when we had the time for it. But, eventually, we realized that hard work and dreams were not enough. Somewhere, in Iowa City maybe, or shortly afterwards, in Sacramento, the dreams began to go bust.

The time came and went when everything my wife and I held sacred, or considered worthy of respect, every spiritual value, crumbled away. Something terrible had happened to us. It was something that we had never seen occur in any other family. We couldn't fully comprehend what had happened. It was erosion, and we couldn't stop it. Somehow, when we weren't looking, the children had got into the driver's seat. As crazy as it sounds now, they held the reins, and the whip. We simply could not have anticipated anything like what was happening to us.

During these ferocious years of parenting, I usually didn't have the time, or the heart, to think about working on anything very lengthy. The circumstances of my life, the "grip and slog" of it, in D.H. Lawrence's phrase, did not permit it. The circumstances of my life with these children dictated something else. They said if I wanted to write anything, and finish it, and if ever I wanted to take satisfaction out of finished work, I was going to have to stick to stories and poems. The short things I could sit down and, with any luck, write quickly and have done with. Very early, long before Iowa City even, I'd understood that I would have a hard time writing a novel, given my anxious inability to focus on anything for a sustained period of time. Looking back on it now, I think I was slowly going nuts with frustration during those ravenous years. Anyway, these circumstances dictated, to the fullest possible extent, the forms my writing could take. God forbid, I'm not complaining now, just giving facts from a heavy and still bewildered heart.

If I'd been able to collect my thoughts and concentrate my energy on a novel, say, I was still in no position to wait for a payoff that, if it came at all, might be several years down the road. I couldn't see the road. I had to sit down and write something I could finish now, tonight, or at least tomorrow night, no later, after I got in from work and before I lost interest. In those days I always worked some crap job or another, and my wife did the same. She waitressed or else was a door-to-door saleswoman. Years later she taught high school. But that was years later. I worked sawmill jobs, janitor jobs, delivery man jobs, service station jobs, stockroom boy jobs—name it, I did it. One summer, in Arcata, California, I picked tulips, I swear, during the daylight hours, to support us; and at night after closing, I cleaned the inside of a drive-in restaurant and swept up the parking lot. Once I even considered, for a few minutes anyway—the job application form there in front of me—becoming a bill collector!

In those days I figured if I could squeeze in an hour or two a day for myself, after job and family, that was more than good enough. That was heaven itself. And I felt happy to have that hour. But sometimes, one reason or another, I couldn't get the hour. Then I would look forward to Saturday, though sometimes things happened that knocked Saturday out as well. But there was Sunday to hope for. Sunday, maybe.

I couldn't see myself working on a novel in such a fashion, that is to say, no fashion at all. To write a novel, it seemed to me, a writer should be living in a world that makes sense, a world that the writer can believe in, draw a bead on, and then write about accurately. A world that will, for a time anyway, stay fixed in one place. Along with this there has to be a belief in the essential *correctness* of that world. A belief that the known world has reasons for existing, and is worth writing about, is not likely to go up in smoke in the process. This wasn't the case with the world I knew and was living in. My world was one that seemed to change gears and directions, along with its rules, every day. Time and again I reached the point where I couldn't see or plan any further ahead than the first of next month and gathering together enough money, by hook or by crook, to meet the rent and provide the children's school clothes. This is true.

I wanted to see tangible results for any so-called literary efforts of mine. No chits or promises, no time certificates, please. So I purposely, and by necessity, limited myself to writing things I knew I could finish in one sitting, two sittings at the most. I'm talking of a first draft now. I've always had patience for rewriting. But in those days I happily looked forward to the rewriting as it took up time which I was glad to have taken up. In one regard I was in no hurry to finish the story or the poem I was working on, for finishing something meant I'd have to find the time, and the belief, to begin something else. So I had great patience with a piece of work after I'd done the initial writing. I'd keep something around the house for what seemed a very long time, fooling with it, changing this, adding that, cutting out something else.

This hit-and-miss way of writing lasted for nearly two decades. There were good times back there, of course; certain grown-up pleasures and satisfactions that only parents have access to. But I'd take poison before I'd go through that time again.

The circumstances of my life are much different now, but now I *choose* to write short stories and poems. Or at least I think I do. Maybe it's all a result of the old writing habits from those days. Maybe I still can't adjust to thinking in terms of having a great swatch of time in which to work on something—anything I want!—and not have to worry about having the chair yanked out from under me, or one of my kids smarting off about why supper isn't ready on demand. But I learned some things along the way. One of the things I learned is that I had to bend or else break. And I also learned that it is possible to bend and break at the same time.

I'll say something about two other individuals who exercised influence on my life. One of them, John Gardner, was teaching a beginning fiction writing course at Chico State College when I signed up for the class in the fall of 1958. My wife and I and the children had just moved down from Yakima, Washington, to a place called Paradise, California, about ten miles up in the foot-hills outside of Chico. We had the promise of low-rent housing and, of course, we thought it would be a great adventure to move to California. (In those days, and for a long while after, we were always up for an adventure.) Of course, I'd have to work to earn a living for us, but I also planned to enroll in college as a part-time student.

Gardner was just out of the University of Iowa with a Ph.D. and, I knew, several unpublished novels and short stories. I'd never met anyone who'd written a novel, published or otherwise. On the first day of class he marched us outside and had us sit on the lawn.

There were six or seven of us, as I recall. He went around, asking us to name the authors we liked to read. I can't remember any names we mentioned, but they must not have been the right names. He announced that he didn't think any of us had what it took to become real writers—as far as he could see none of us had the necessary *fire*. But he said he was going to do what he could for us, though it was obvious he didn't expect much to come of it. But there was an implication too that we were about to set off on a trip, and we'd do well to hold onto our hats.

I remember at another class meeting he said he wasn't going to mention any of the big-circulation magazines except to sneer at them. He'd brought in a stack of "little" magazines, the literary quarterlies, and he told us to read the work in those magazines. He told us that this was where the best fiction in the country was being published, and all of the poetry. He said he was there to tell us which authors to read as well as teach us how to write. He was amazingly arrogant. He gave us a list of the little magazines he thought were worth something, and he went down the list with us and talked a little about each magazine. Of course, none of us had ever heard of these magazines. It was the first I'd ever known of their existence. I remember him saying during this time, it might have been during a conference, that writers were made as well as born. (Is this true? My God, I still don't know. I suppose every writer who teaches creative writing and who takes the job at all seriously has to believe this to some extent. There are apprentice musicians and composers and visual artists—so why *not* writers?) I was impressionable then, I suppose I still am, but I was terrifically impressed with everything he said and did. He'd take one of my early efforts at a story and go over it with me. I remember him as being very patient, wanting me to understand what he was trying to show me, telling me over and over how important it was to have the right words saying what I wanted them to say. Nothing vague or blurred, no smoked-glass prose. And he kept drumming at me the importance of using—I don't know how else to say it—common language, the language of normal discourse, the language we speak to each other in.

Recently we had dinner together in Ithaca, New York, and I reminded him then of some of the sessions we'd had up in his office. He answered that probably everything he'd told me was wrong. He said, "I've changed my mind about so many things." All I know is that the advice he was handing out in those days was just what I needed at that time. He was a wonderful teacher. It was a great thing to have happen to me at that period of my life, to have someone who took me seriously enough to sit down and go over a manuscript with me. I knew something crucial was happening to me, something that mattered. He helped me to see how important it was to say exactly what I wanted to say and nothing else; not to use "literary" words or "pseudo-poetic" language. He'd try to explain to me the difference between saying something like, for example, "wing of a meadow lark" and "meadow lark's wing." There's a different sound and feel, yes? The word "ground" and the word "earth," for instance. Ground is ground, he'd say, it means *ground*, dirt, that kind of stuff. But if you say "earth" that's something else, that word has other ramifications. He taught me to use contractions in my writing. He helped show me how to say what I wanted to say and to use the minimum number of words to do so. He made me see that absolutely everything was important in a short story. It was of consequence where the commas and periods went. For this, for that—for his giving me the key to his office so I would have a place to write on the weekends—for his putting up with my brashness and general nonsense, I'll always be grateful. He was an influence.

Ten years later I was still alive, still living with my children, still writing an occasional story or poem. I sent one of the occasional stories to *Esquire* and in so doing hoped to be able to forget about it for a while. But the story came back by return mail, along with a letter from Gordon Lish, at that time the fiction editor for the magazine. He said he was returning the story. He was not apologizing that he was returning it, not returning it "reluctantly," he was just returning it. But he asked to see others. So I promptly sent him everything I had, and he just as promptly sent everything back. But again a friendly letter accompanied the work I'd sent to him.

At that time, the early 1970s, I was living in Palo Alto with my family. I was in my early thirties and I had my first white-collar job

—I was an editor for a textbook publishing firm. We lived in a house that had an old garage out back. The previous tenants had built a playroom in the garage, and I'd go out to this garage every night I could manage after dinner and try to write something. If I couldn't write anything, and this was often the case, I'd just sit in there for a while by myself, thankful to be away from the fracas that always seemed to be raging inside the house. But I was writing a short story that I'd called "The Neighbors." I finally finished the story and sent it off to Lish. A letter came back almost immediately telling me how much he liked it, that he was changing the title to "Neighbors," that he was recommending to the magazine that the story be purchased. It was purchased, it did appear, and nothing, it seemed to me, would ever be the same. *Esquire* soon bought another story, and then another, and so on. James Dickey became poetry editor of the magazine during this time, and he began accepting my poems for publication. In one regard, things had never seemed better. But my kids were in full cry then, like the race track crowd I can hear at this moment, and they were eating me alive. My life soon took another veering, a sharp turn, and then it came to a dead stop off on a siding. I couldn't go anywhere, couldn't back up or go forward. It was during this period that Lish collected some of my stories and gave them to McGraw-Hill, who published them. For the time being, I was still off on the siding, unable to move in any direction. If there'd once been a fire, it'd gone out.

Influences. John Gardner and Gordon Lish. They hold irredeemable notes. But my children are it. Theirs is the main influence. They were the prime movers and shapers of my life and my writing. As you can see, I'm still under their influence, though the days are relatively clear now, and the silences are right.

POEMS

ONE

DRINKING WHILE DRIVING

It's August and I have not
read a book in six months
except something called *The Retreat From Moscow*
by Caulaincourt.
Nevertheless, I am happy
riding in a car with my brother
and drinking from a pint of Old Crow.
We do not have any place in mind to go,
we are just driving.
If I closed my eyes for a minute
I would be lost, yet
I could gladly lie down and sleep forever
beside this road.
My brother nudges me.
Any minute now, something will happen.

LUCK

I was nine years old.
I had been around liquor
all my life. My friends
drank too, but they could handle it.
We'd take cigarettes, beer,
a couple of girls
and go out to the fort.
We'd act silly.
Sometimes you'd pretend
to pass out so the girls
could examine you.
They'd put their hands
down your pants while
you lay there trying
not to laugh, or else
they would lean back,
close their eyes, and
let you feel them all over.
Once at a party my dad
came to the back porch
to take a leak.
We could hear voices
over the record player,
see people standing around
laughing and drinking.
When my dad finished
he zipped up, stared a while
at the starry sky—it was
always starry then
on summer nights—
and went back inside.
The girls had to go home.

I slept all night in the fort
with my best friend.
We kissed on the lips
and touched each other.
I saw the stars fade
toward morning.
I saw a woman sleeping
on our lawn.
I looked up her dress,
then I had a beer
and a cigarette.
Friends, I thought this
was living.
Indoors, someone
had put out a cigarette
in a jar of mustard.
I had a straight shot
from the bottle, then
a drink of warm collins mix,
then another whisky.
And though I went from room
to room, no one was home.
What luck, I thought.
Years later,
I still wanted to give up
friends, love, starry skies,
for a house where no one
was home, no one coming back,
and all I could drink.

DISTRESS SALE

Early one Sunday morning everything outside—
the child's canopy bed and vanity table,
the sofa, end tables and lamps, boxes
of assorted books and records. We carried out
kitchen items, a clock radio, hanging
clothes, a big easy chair
with them from the beginning
and which they called Uncle.
Lastly, we brought out the kitchen table itself
and they set up around that to do business.
The sky promises to hold fair.
I'm staying here with them, trying to dry out.
I slept on that canopy bed last night.
This business is hard on us all.
It's Sunday and they hope to catch the trade
from the Episcopal church next door.
What a situation here! What disgrace!
Everyone who sees this collection of junk
on the sidewalk is bound to be mortified.
The woman, a family member, a loved one,
a woman who once wanted to be an actress,
she chats with fellow parishioners who
smile awkwardly and finger items
of clothing before moving on.
The man, my friend, sits at the table
and tries to look interested in what
he's reading—Froissart's *Chronicles* it is,
I can see it from the window.
My friend is finished, done for, and he knows it.
What's going on here? Can no one help them?
Must everyone witness their downfall?
This reduces us all.
Someone must show up at once to save them,

to take everything off their hands right now,
every trace of this life before
this humiliation goes on any longer.
Someone must do something.
I reach for my wallet and that is how I understand it:
I can't help anyone.

YOUR DOG DIES

it gets run over by a van.
you find it at the side of the road
and bury it.
you feel bad about it.
you feel bad personally,
but you feel bad for your daughter
because it was her pet,
and she loved it so.
she used to croon to it
and let it sleep in her bed.
you write a poem about it.
you call it a poem for your daughter,
about the dog getting run over by a van
and how you looked after it,
took it out into the woods
and buried it deep, deep,
and that poem turns out so good
you're almost glad the little dog
was run over, or else you'd never
have written that good poem.
then you sit down to write
a poem about writing a poem
about the death of that dog,
but while you're writing you
hear a woman scream
your name, your first name,
both syllables,
and your heart stops.
after a minute, you continue writing.
she screams again.
you wonder how long this can go on.

PHOTOGRAPH OF MY FATHER
IN HIS TWENTY-SECOND YEAR

October. Here in this dank, unfamiliar kitchen
I study my father's embarrassed young man's face.
Sheepish grin, he holds in one hand a string
of spiny yellow perch, in the other
a bottle of Carlsbad beer.

In jeans and denim shirt, he leans
against the front fender of a 1934 Ford.
He would like to pose bluff and hearty for his posterity,
wear his old hat cocked over his ear.
All his life my father wanted to be bold.

But the eyes give him away, and the hands
that limply offer the string of dead perch
and the bottle of beer. Father, I love you,
yet how can I say thank you, I who can't hold my liquor either,
and don't even know the places to fish?

HAMID RAMOUZ (1818–1906)

This morning I began a poem on Hamid Ramouz—
soldier, scholar, desert explorer—
who died by his own hand, gunshot, at eighty-eight.

I had tried to read the dictionary entry on that curious man
to my son—we were after something on Raleigh—
but he was impatient, and rightly so.

It happened months ago, the boy is with his mother now,
but I remembered the name: Ramouz—
and a poem began to take shape.

All morning I sat at the table,
hands moving back and forth over limitless waste,
as I tried to recall that strange life.

BANKRUPTCY

Twenty-eight, hairy belly hanging out
of my undershirt (exempt)
I lie here on my side
on the couch (exempt)
and listen to the strange sound
of my wife's pleasant voice (also exempt).

We are new arrivals
to these small pleasures.
Forgive me (I pray the Court)
that we have been improvident.
Today, my heart, like the front door,
stands open for the first time in months.

THE BAKER

Then Pancho Villa came to town,
hanged the mayor
and summoned the old and infirm
Count Vronsky to supper.
Pancho introduced his new girl friend,
along with her husband in his white apron,
showed Vronsky his pistol,
then asked the Count to tell him
about his unhappy exile in Mexico.
Later, the talk was of women and horses.
Both were experts.
The girl friend giggled
and fussed with the pearl buttons
on Pancho's shirt until,
promptly at midnight, Pancho went to sleep
with his head on the table.
The husband crossed himself
and left the house holding his boots
without so much as a sign
to his wife or Vronsky.
That anonymous husband, barefooted,
humiliated, trying to save his life, he
is the hero of this poem.

IOWA SUMMER

The paperboy shakes me awake. "I have been dreaming you'd
    come,"
I tell him, rising from the bed. He is accompanied
by a giant Negro from the university who seems
itching to get his hands on me. I stall for time.
Sweat runs off our faces; we stand waiting.
I do not offer them chairs and no one speaks.

It is only later, after they've gone,
I realize they have delivered a letter.
It's a letter from my wife. "What are you doing
there?" my wife asks. "Are you drinking?"
I study the postmark for hours. Then it, too, begins to fade.
I hope someday to forget all this.

ALCOHOL

That painting next to the brocaded drapery
is a Delacroix. This is called a divan
not a davenport; this item is a settee.
Notice the ornate legs.
Put on your tarboosh. Smell the burnt cork
under your eyes. Adjust your tunic, so.
Now the red cummerbund and Paris; April 1934.
A black Citröen waits at the curb.
The street lamps are lit.
Give the driver the address, but tell him
not to hurry, that you have all night.
When you get there, drink, make love,
do the shimmy and the beguine.
And when the sun comes up over the Quarter
next morning and that pretty woman
you've had and had all night
now wants to go home with you,
be tender with her, don't do anything
you'll be sorry for later. Bring her home
with you in the Citröen, let her sleep
in a proper bed. Let her
fall in love with you and you
with her and then...something: alcohol,
a problem with alcohol, always alcohol—
what you've really done
and to someone else, the one
you meant to love from the start.

It's afternoon, August, sun striking
the hood of a dusty Ford
parked on your driveway in San Jose.
In the front seat a woman
who is covering her eyes and listening

to an old song on the radio.
You stand in the doorway and watch.
You hear the song. And it is long ago.
You look for it with the sun in your face.
But you don't remember.
You honestly don't remember.

FOR SEMRA, WITH MARTIAL VIGOR

How much do writers make? she said
first off
she'd never met a writer
before
Not much I said
they have to do other things as well
Like what? she said
Like working in mills I said
sweeping floors teaching school
picking fruit
whatnot
all kinds of things I said
In my country she said
someone who has been to college
would never sweep floors
Well that's just when they're starting out I said
all writers make lots of money
Write me a poem she said
a love poem
All poems are love poems I said
I don't understand she said
It's hard to explain I said
Write it for me now she said
All right I said
a napkin/a pencil
for Semra I wrote
Not now silly she said
nibbling my shoulder
I just wanted to see
Later? I said
putting my hand on her thigh
Later she said

O Semra Semra
Next to Paris she said
Istanbul is the loveliest city
Have you read Omar Khayyam? she said
Yes yes I said
a loaf of bread a flask of wine
I know Omar backwards
& forwards
Kahlil Gibran? she said
Who? I said
Gibran she said
Not exactly I said
What do you think of the military? she said
have you been in the military?
No I said
I don't think much of the military
Why not? she said
goddamn don't you think men
should go in the military?
Well of course I said
they should
I lived with a man once she said
a real man a captain
in the army
but he was killed
Well hell I said
looking around for a saber
drunk as a post
damn their eyes retreat hell
I just got here
the teapot flying across the table
I'm sorry I said

to the teapot
Semra I mean
Hell she said
I don't know why the hell
I let you pick me up

LOOKING FOR WORK

I've always wanted brook trout
for breakfast.

Suddenly, I find a new path
to the waterfall.

I begin to hurry.
Wake up,

my wife says,
you're dreaming.

But when I try to rise,
the house tilts.

Who's dreaming?
It's noon, she says.

My new shoes wait by the door.
They are gleaming.

CHEERS

Vodka chased with coffee. Each morning
I hang the sign on the door:

OUT TO LUNCH

but no one pays attention; my friends
look at the sign and
sometimes leave little notes,
or else they call—*Come out and play,
Ray-mond.*

Once my son, that bastard,
slipped in and left me a colored egg
and a walking stick.
I think he drank some of my vodka.
And last week my wife dropped by
with a can of beef soup
and a carton of tears.
She drank some of my vodka, too, I think,
then left hurriedly in a strange car
with a man I'd never seen before.
They don't understand; I'm fine,
just fine where I am, for any day now
I shall be, I shall be, I shall be...

I intend to take all the time in this world,
consider everything, even miracles,
yet remain on guard, ever
more careful, more watchful,
against those who would sin against me,
against those who would steal vodka,
against those who would do me harm.

ROGUE RIVER JET-BOAT TRIP,
GOLD BEACH, OREGON, JULY 4, 1977

They promised an unforgettable trip,
deer, marten, osprey, the site
of the Mick Smith massacre—
a man who slaughtered his family,
who burnt his house down around his ears—
a fried chicken dinner.
I am not drinking. For this
you have put on your wedding ring and driven
500 miles to see for yourself.
This light dazzles. I fill my lungs
as if these last years
were nothing, a little overnight portage.
We sit in the bow of the jet-boat
and you make small talk with the guide.
He asks where we're from, but seeing
our confusion, becomes
confused himself and tells us
he has a glass eye and we
should try to guess which is which.
His good eye, the left, is brown, is
steady of purpose, and doesn't
miss a thing. Not long past
I would have snagged it out
just for its warmth, youth, and purpose,
and because it lingers on your breasts.
Now, I no longer know what's mine, what
isn't. I no longer know anything except
I am not drinking—though I'm still weak
and sick from it. The engine starts.
The guide attends the wheel.
Spray rises and falls on all sides
as we head upriver.

TWO

YOU DON'T KNOW WHAT LOVE IS
(an evening with Charles Bukowski)

You don't know what love is Bukowski said
I'm 51 years old look at me
I'm in love with this young broad
I got it bad but she's hung up too
so it's all right man that's the way it should be
I get in their blood and they can't get me out
They try everything to get away from me
but they all come back in the end
They all came back to me except
the one I planted
I cried over that one
but I cried easy in those days
Don't let me get onto the hard stuff man
I get mean then
I could sit here and drink beer
with you hippies all night
I could drink ten quarts of this beer
and nothing it's like water
But let me get onto the hard stuff
and I'll start throwing people out windows
I'll throw anybody out the window
I've done it
But you don't know what love is
You don't know because you've never
been in love it's that simple
I got this young broad see she's beautiful
She calls me Bukowski
Bukowski she says in this little voice
and I say What
But you don't know what love is
I'm telling you what it is
but you aren't listening

There isn't one of you in this room
would recognize love if it stepped up
and buggered you in the ass
I used to think poetry readings were a copout
Look I'm 51 years old and I've been around
I *know* they're a copout
but I said to myself Bukowski
starving is even more of a copout
So there you are and nothing is like it should be
That fellow what's his name Galway Kinnell
I saw his picture in a magazine
He has a handsome mug on him
but he's a *teacher*
Christ can you imagine
But then you're teachers too
here I am insulting you already
No I haven't heard of him
or him either
They're all termites
Maybe it's ego I don't read much anymore
but these people who build
reputations on five or six books
termites
Bukowski she says
Why do you listen to classical music all day
Can't you hear her saying that
Bukowski why do you listen to classical music all day
That surprises you doesn't it
You wouldn't think a crude bastard like me
could listen to classical music all day
Brahms Rachmaninoff Bartok Telemann
Shit I couldn't write up here
Too quiet up here too many trees

I like the city that's the place for me
I put on my classical music each morning
and sit down in front of my typewriter
I light a cigar and I smoke it like this see
and I say Bukowski you're a lucky man
Bukowski you've gone through it all
and you're a lucky man
and the blue smoke drifts across the table
and I look out the window onto Delongpre Avenue
and I see people walking up and down the sidewalk
and I puff on the cigar like this
and then I lay the cigar in the ashtray like this
and take a deep breath
and I begin to write
Bukowski this is the life I say
it's good to be poor it's good to have hemorrhoids
it's good to be in love
But you don't know what it's like
You don't know what it's like to be in love
If you could see her you'd know what I mean
She thought I'd come up here and get laid
She just knew it
She told me she knew it
Shit I'm 51 years old and she's 25
and we're in love and she's jealous
Jesus it's beautiful
she said she'd claw my eyes out if I came up here and
        got laid
Now that's love for you
What do any of you know about it
Let me tell you something
I've met men in jail who had more style
than the people who hang around colleges

and go to poetry readings
They're bloodsuckers who come to see
if the poet's socks are dirty
or if he smells under the arms
Believe me I won't disappoint em
But I want you to remember this
there's only one poet in this room tonight
only one poet in this town tonight
maybe only one real poet in this country tonight
and that's me
What do any of you know about life
What do any of you know about anything
Which of you here has been fired from a job
or else has beaten up your broad
or else has been beaten up by your broad
I was fired from Sears and Roebuck five times
They'd fire me then hire me back again
I was a stockboy for them when I was 35
and then got canned for stealing cookies
I know what's it like I've been there
I'm 51 years old now and I'm in love
This little broad she says
Bukowski
and I say What and she says
I think you're full of shit
and I say baby you understand me
She's the only broad in the world
man or woman
I'd take that from
But you don't know what love is
They all came back to me in the end too
every one of em came back
except that one I told you about

the one I planted
We were together seven years
We used to drink a lot
I see a couple of typers in this room but
I don't see any poets
I'm not surprised
You have to have been in love to write poetry
and you don't know what it is to be in love
that's your trouble
Give me some of that stuff
That's right no ice good
That's good that's just fine
So let's get this show on the road
I know what I said but I'll have just one
That tastes good
Okay then let's go let's get this over with
only afterwards don't anyone stand close
to an open window

THREE

MORNING, THINKING OF EMPIRE

We press our lips to the enameled rim of the cups
and know this grease that floats
over the coffee will one day stop our hearts.
Eyes and fingers drop onto silverware
that is not silverware. Outside the window, waves
beat against the chipped walls of the old city.
Your hands rise from the rough tablecloth
as if to prophesy. Your lips tremble...
I want to say to hell with the future.
Our future lies deep in the afternoon.
It is a narrow street with a cart and driver,
a driver who looks at us and hesitates,
then shakes his head. Meanwhile,
I coolly crack the egg of a fine Leghorn chicken.
Your eyes film. You turn from me and look across
the rooftops at the sea. Even the flies are still.
I crack the other egg.
Surely we have diminished one another.

THE BLUE STONES

*If I call stones blue it is because
blue is the precise word, believe me.*
                                        —FLAUBERT

You are writing a love scene
between Emma Bovary and Rodolphe Boulanger,
but love has nothing to do with it.
You are writing about sexual desire,
that longing of one person to possess another
whose ultimate aim is penetration.
Love has nothing to do with it.
You write and write that scene
until you arouse yourself,
masturbate into a handkerchief.
Still, you don't get up from the desk
for hours. You go on writing that scene,
writing about hunger, blind energy—
the very nature of sex—
a fiery leaning into consequence
and eventually, utter ruin
if unbridled. And sex,
what is sex if it is not unbridled?

You walk on the strand that night
with your magpie friend, Ed Goncourt.
You tell him when you write
love scenes these days you can jackoff
without leaving your desk.
"Love has nothing to do with it," you say.
You enjoy a cigar and a clear view of Jersey.
The tide is going out across the shingle,
and nothing on earth can stop it.

The smooth stones you pick up and examine
under the moon's light have been made blue
from the sea. Next morning when you pull them
from your trouser pocket, they are still blue.

—*for my wife*

TEL AVIV AND *LIFE ON THE MISSISSIPPI*

This afternoon the Mississippi—
high, roily under a broiling sun,
or low, rippling under starlight,
set with deadly snags come out to fish
for steamboats—
the Mississippi this afternoon
has never seemed so far away.

Plantations pass in the darkness;
there's Jones's landing appearing out
of nowhere, out of pine trees,
and here at 12-Mile Point, Gray's
overseer reaches out of fog and receives
a packet of letters, souvenirs and such
from New Orleans.

Bixby, that pilot you loved,
fumes and burns:
D--nation, boy! he storms at you time and again.
Vicksburg, Memphis, St. Looey, Cincinnati,
the paddleblades flash and rush, rush
upriver, soughing and churning
the dark water.

Mark Twain you're all eyes and ears,
you're taking all this down to tell later,
everything,
even how you got your name,
quarter twain, mark twain,
something every schoolboy knew
save one.

I hang my legs further over the banister
and lean back in shade,
holding to the book like a wheel,
sweating, fooling my life away,
as some children haggle,
then fiercely slap each other
in the field below.

THE NEWS CARRIED TO MACEDONIA

On the banks of the
        river they call Indus today
we observe a kind of
bean
        much like the Egyptian bean
        also
crocodiles are reported
upstream & hillsides grown over
        with myrrh & ivy
                He believes
we have located the headwaters
of the River Nile
        we offer
sacrifice
hold games
        for the occasion
There is much rejoicing &
                the men think
        we shall turn back
These elephants their
emissaries offer
        are giant
terrifying beasts yet
        with a grin he yesterday
ran up a ladder onto
        the very top of one
        beast
The men
                cheered him & he
waved & they cheered him
        again
He pointed across the river
        & the men grew silent

The builders
busy themselves with great rafts
    at the water's edge
        on the morrow
we again set our faces
    to the East
Tonight
        wind   birds
fill the air
    the clacking of their bills
like iron on iron
The wind
        is steady is fragrant
    with jasmine
trail of the country behind us
The wind moves
        through the camp
stirs the tents of
the Hetaeri
        touches each
of the sleeping soldiers
Euoi! Euoi!
    men cry out
in their sleep & the horses
        prick their ears & stand
    shivering
In a few hours
they all shall wake
    with the sun
shall follow the wind
        even further

THE MOSQUE IN JAFFA

I lean over the balcony of the minaret.
My head swims.
A few steps away the man who intends
to betray me begins by pointing out
key sights—
market church prison whorehouse.
Killed, he says.
Words lost in the wind but
drawing a finger across his throat
so I will get it.
He grins.
The key words fly out—
Turks Greeks Arabs Jews
trade worship love murder
a beautiful woman.
He grins again at such foolishness.
He knows I am watching him.
Still he whistles confidently
as we start down the steps
bumping against each other going down
commingling breath and bodies in the narrow
spiralling dark.
Downstairs, his friends are waiting
with a car. We all of us light cigarettes
and think what to do next.
Time, like the light in his dark eyes,
is running out as we climb in.

NOT FAR FROM HERE

Not far from here someone
is calling my name.
I jump to the floor.

Still, this could be a trap.
Careful, careful.
I look under the covers for my knife.

But even as I curse God
for the delay, the door is thrown open
and a long-haired brat enters

carrying a dog.
What is it, child? (We are both
trembling.) What do you want?

But the tongue only hops and flutters
in her open mouth
as a single sound rises in her throat.

I move closer, kneel
and place my ear against the tiny lips.
When I stand up—the dog grins.

Listen, I don't have time for games.
Here, I say, here—and I send her away
with a plum.

SUDDEN RAIN

●

Rain hisses onto stones as old men and women
drive donkeys to cover.
We stand in rain, more foolish than donkeys,
and shout, walk up and down in rain and accuse.

●

When rain stops the old men and women
who have waited quietly in doorways, smoking,
lead their donkeys out once more and up the hill.

●

Behind, always behind, I climb through the narrow
        streets.
I roll my eyes. I clatter against stones.

BALZAC

I think of Balzac in his nightcap after
thirty hours at his writing desk,
mist rising from his face,
the gown clinging
to his hairy thighs as
he scratches himself, lingers
at the open window.
Outside, on the boulevards,
the plump white hands of the creditors
stroke moustaches and cravats,
young ladies dream of Chateaubriand
and promenade with the young men, while
empty carriages rattle by, smelling
of axle-grease and leather.
Like a huge draught horse, Balzac
yawns, snorts, lumbers
to the watercloset
and, flinging open his gown,
trains a great stream of piss into the
early nineteenth century
chamberpot. The lace curtain catches
the breeze. Wait! One last scene
before sleep. His brain sizzles as
he goes back to his desk—the pen,
the pot of ink, the strewn pages.

COUNTRY MATTERS

A girl pushes a bicycle through tall grass,
through overturned garden furniture, water
rising to her ankles. Cups without handles
sail upon the murky water, saucers
with fine cracks in the porcelain.
At the upstairs window, behind damask curtains,
the steward's pale blue eyes follow.
He tries to call.
Shreds of yellow note paper
float out onto the wintry air, but the girl
does not turn her head.
Cook is away, no one hears.
Then two fists appear on the window sill.
He leans closer to hear the small
whisperings, the broken story, the excuses.

THIS ROOM

This room for instance:
is that an empty coach
that waits below?

     Promises, promises,
     tell them nothing
     for my sake.

I remember parasols,
an esplanade beside the sea,
yet these flowers...

     Must I ever remain behind—
     listening, smoking,
     scribbling down the next far thing?

I light a cigarette
and adjust the window shade.
There is a noise in the street
growing fainter, fainter.

RHODES

•

I don't know the names of flowers
or one tree from another,
nevertheless I sit in the square
under a cloud of Papisostros smoke
and sip Hellas beer.
Somewhere nearby there is a Colossus
waiting for another artist,
another earthquake.
But I'm not ambitious.
I'd like to stay, it's true,
though I'd want to hang out
with the civic deer that surround
the Hospitaler castle on the hill.
They are beautiful deer
and their lean haunches flicker
under an assault of white butterflies.

•

High on the battlement a tall, stiff
figure of a man keeps watch on Turkey.
A warm rain begins to fall.
A peacock shakes drops of water
from its tail and heads for cover.
In the Moslem graveyard a cat sleeps
in a niche between two stones.
Just time for a look
into the casino, except
I'm not dressed.

Back on board, ready for bed,
I lie down and remember
I've been to Rhodes.
But there's something else—
I hear again the voice
of the croupier calling
thirty-two, thirty-two
as my body flies over water,
as my soul, poised like a cat, hovers—
then leaps into sleep.

SPRING, 480 B.C.

Enraged by what he called
    the impertinence of the Hellespont
        in blowing up a storm
    which brought to a halt
        his army of 2 million,
            Herodotus relates
    that Xerxes ordered 300
        lashes be given
    that unruly body of water besides
    throwing in a pair of fetters, followed
        by a branding with hot irons.
You can imagine
    how this news was received
            at Athens; I mean
    that the Persians were on the march.

FOUR

NEAR KLAMATH

We stand around the burning oil drum
and we warm ourselves, our hands
and faces, in its pure lapping heat.

We raise steaming cups of coffee
to our lips and we drink it
with both hands. But we are salmon

fishermen. And now we stamp our feet
on the snow and rocks and move upstream,
slowly, full of love, toward the still pools.

AUTUMN

This yardful of the landlord's used cars
does not intrude. The landlord
himself, does not intrude. He hunches
all day over a swage,
or else is enveloped in the blue flame
of the arc-welding device.
        He takes note of me though,
often stopping work to grin
and nod at me through the window. He even
apologizes for parking his logging gear
in my living room.
        But we remain friends.
Slowly the days thin, and we
move together towards spring,
towards high water, the jack-salmon,
the sea-run cutthroat.

WINTER INSOMNIA

The mind can't sleep, can only lie awake and
gorge, listening to the snow gather as
for some final assault.

It wishes Chekov were here to minister
something—three drops of valerian, a glass
of rose water—anything, it wouldn't matter.

The mind would like to get out of here
onto the snow. It would like to run
with a pack of shaggy animals, all teeth,

under the moon, across the snow, leaving
no prints or spoor, nothing behind.
The mind is sick tonight.

PROSSER

In winter two kinds of fields on the hills
outside Prosser: fields of new green wheat, the slips
rising overnight out of the plowed ground,
and waiting,
and then rising again, and budding.
Geese love this green wheat.
I ate some of it once too, to see.

And wheat stubble-fields that reach to the river.
These are the fields that have lost everything.
At night they try to recall their youth,
but their breathing is slow and irregular as
their life sinks into dark furrows.
Geese love this shattered wheat also.
They will die for it.

But everything is forgotten, nearly everything,
and sooner rather than later, please God—
fathers, friends, they pass
into your life and out again, a few women stay
a while, then go, and the fields
turn their backs, disappear in rain.
Everything goes, but Prosser.

Those nights driving back through miles of wheat
          fields—
headlamps raking the fields on the curves—
Prosser, that town, shining as we break over hills,
heater rattling, tired through to bone,
the smell of gunpowder on our fingers still:
I can barely see him, my father, squinting
through the windshield of that cab, saying, Prosser.

AT NIGHT THE SALMON MOVE

At night the salmon move
out from the river and into town.
They avoid places with names
like Foster's Freeze, A&W, Smiley's,
but swim close to the tract
homes on Wright Avenue where sometimes
in the early morning hours
you can hear them trying doorknobs
or bumping against Cable TV lines.
We wait up for them.
We leave our back windows open
and call out when we hear a splash.
Mornings are a disappointment.

WITH A TELESCOPE ROD
ON COWICHE CREEK

Here my assurance drops away.   I lose
all direction.   Gray Lady
onto moving waters.   My thoughts
stir like ruffed grouse
in the clearing across the creek.

Suddenly, as at a signal, the birds
pass silently back into pine trees.

POEM FOR DR. PRATT,
A LADY PATHOLOGIST

●

Last night I dreamt a priest came to me
holding in his hands white bones,
white bones in his white hands.
He was gentle,
not like Father McCormick with his webbed fingers.
I was not frightened.

●

This afternoon the maids come with their mops
and disinfectant. They pretend I'm not
there, talk of menstrual cycles as they
push my bed this way and that. Before leaving,
they embrace. Gradually, the room
fills with leaves. I am afraid.

●

The window is open. Sunlight.
Across the room a bed creaks, creaks
under the weight of lovemaking.
The man clears his throat. Outside,
I hear sprinklers. I begin to void.
A green desk floats by the window.

●

My heart lies on the table, a parody
of affection, while her fingers rummage
the endless string of entrails.
These considerations aside,
after all those years of adventure in the Far East,
I am in love with these hands, but
I'm cold beyond imagining.

WES HARDIN: FROM A PHOTOGRAPH

Turning through a collection
    of old photographs
I come to a picture of the outlaw,
    Wes Hardin, dead.
He is a big, moustached man
    in a black suitcoat
on his back over a boardfloor
    in Amarillo, Texas.
His head is turned at the camera
    and his face
seems bruised, the hair
    jarred loose.
A bullet has entered his skull
    from behind
coming out a little hole
    over his right eye.

Nothing so funny about that
    but three shabby men
in overalls stand grinning
    a few feet away.
They are all holding rifles
    and that one
at the end has on what must be
    the outlaw's hat.
Several other bullets are dotted
    here and there
under the fancy white shirt
    the deceased is wearing
—in a manner of speaking—

but what makes me stare
is this large dark bullethole
through the slender, delicate-looking
right hand.

MARRIAGE

In our cabin we eat breaded oysters and fries
with lemon cookies for dessert, as the marriage
of Kitty and Levin unfolds on Public TV.
The man in the trailer up the hill, our neighbor,
has just gotten out of jail again.
This morning he drove into the yard with his wife
in a big yellow car, radio blaring.
His wife turned off the radio while he parked,
and together they walked slowly
to their trailer without saying anything.
It was early morning, birds were out.
Later, he propped open the door
with a chair to let in spring air and light.

It's Easter Sunday night,
and Kitty and Levin are married at last.
It's enough to bring tears to the eyes, that marriage
and all the lives it touched. We go on
eating oysters, watching television,
remarking on the fine clothes and amazing grace
of the people caught up in this story, some of them
straining under the pressures of adultery,
separation from loved ones, and the destruction
they must know lies in store just after
the next cruel turn of circumstance, and then the
        next.

A dog barks. I get up to check the door.
Behind the curtains are trailers and a muddy
parking area with cars. The moon sails west
as I watch, armed to the teeth, hunting
for my children. My neighbor,
liquored up now, starts his big car, races

the engine, and heads out again, filled
with confidence. The radio wails,
beats something out. When he has gone
there are only the little ponds of silver water
that shiver and can't understand their being here.

THE OTHER LIFE

> *Now for the other life. The one*
> *without mistakes.*
>   —LOU LIPSITZ

My wife is in the other half of this mobile home
making a case against me.
I can hear her pen *scratch, scratch.*
Now and then she stops to weep,
then—*scratch, scratch.*

The frost is going out of the ground.
The man who owns this unit tells me,
Don't leave your car here.
My wife goes on writing and weeping,
weeping and writing in our new kitchen.

THE MAILMAN AS CANCER PATIENT

Hanging around the house each day
the mailman never smiles; he tires
easily, is losing weight,
that's all; they'll hold the job—
besides, he needed a rest.
He will not hear it discussed.

As he walks the empty rooms, he
thinks of crazy things
like Tommy and Jimmy Dorsey,
shaking hands with Franklin D. Roosevelt
at Grand Coulee Dam,
New Year's Eve parties he liked best;
enough things to fill a book
he tells his wife, who
also thinks crazy things
yet keeps on working.
But sometimes at night
the mailman dreams he rises from his bed
puts on his clothes and goes
out, trembling with joy...

He hates those dreams
for when he wakes
there's nothing left; it is
as if he'd never been
anywhere, never done anything;
there is just the room,
the early morning without sun,
the sound of a doorknob
turning slowly.

POEM FOR HEMINGWAY
& W.C. WILLIAMS

3 fat trout hang
        in the still pool
below the new
        steel bridge.
two friends
        come slowly up
the track.
        one of them,
ex-heavyweight,
        wears an old
hunting cap.
        he wants to kill,
that is catch & eat,
        the fish.
the other,
        medical man,
he knows the chances
        of that.
he thinks it fine
        that they should
simply hang there
        always
in the clear water.
        the two keep going
but they
        discuss it as
they disappear
        into the fading trees
& fields & light,
        upstream.

TORTURE

—for *Stephen Dobyns*

You are falling in love again. This time
it is a South American general's daughter.
You want to be stretched on the rack again.
You want to hear awful things said to you
and to admit these things are true.
You want to have unspeakable acts
committed against your person, things
nice people don't talk about in classrooms.
You want to tell everything you know
on Simon Bolivar, on Jorge Luis Borges,
on yourself most of all.
You want to implicate everyone in this!
Even when it's four o'clock in the morning
and the lights are burning still—
those lights that have been burning night and day
in your eyes and brain for two weeks—
and you are dying for a smoke and a lemonade,
but she won't turn off the lights that woman
with the green eyes and little ways about her,
even then you want to be her gaucho.
Dance with me, you imagine hearing her say
as you reach for the empty beaker of water.
Dance with me, she says again and no mistake.
She picks this minute to ask you, hombre,
to get up and dance with her in the nude.
No, you don't have the strength of a fallen leaf,
not the strength of a little reed basket
battered by waves on Lake Titicaca.
But you bound out of bed
just the same, amigo, you dance
across wide open spaces.

BOBBER

On the Columbia River near Vantage,
Washington, we fished for whitefish
in the winter months; my dad, Swede—
Mr. Lindgren—and me. They used belly-reels,
pencil-length sinkers, red, yellow, or brown
flies baited with maggots.
They wanted distance and went clear out there
to the edge of the riffle.
I fished near shore with a quill bobber and a cane pole.

My dad kept his maggots alive and warm
under his lower lip. Mr. Lindgren didn't drink.
I liked him better than my dad for a time.
He let me steer his car, teased me
about my name "Junior," and said
one day I'd grow into a fine man, remember
all this, and fish with my own son.
But my dad was right. I mean
he kept silent and looked into the river,
worked his tongue, like a thought, behind the bait.

HIGHWAY 99E FROM CHICO

The mallard ducks are down
for the night. They chuckle
in their sleep and dream of Mexico
and Honduras. Watercress
nods in the irrigation ditch
and the tules slump forward, heavy
with blackbirds.

Rice fields float under the moon.
Even the wet maple leaves cling
to my windshield. I tell you Maryann,
I am happy.

THE COUGAR

—*for John Haines and Keith Wilson*

I stalked a cougar once in a lost box-canyon
off the Columbia River gorge near the town and river
of Klickitat. We were loaded for grouse. October,
gray sky reaching over into Oregon, and beyond,
all the way to California. None of us had been there,
to California, but we knew about that place—they had
restaurants
that let you fill your plate as many times as you wanted.

I stalked a cougar that day,
if stalk is the right word, clumping and scraping along
upwind of the cougar, smoking cigarettes too,
one after the other, a nervous, fat, sweating kid
under the best of circumstances, but that day
I stalked a cougar..

And then I was weaving drunk there in the living room,
fumbling to put it into words, smacked and scattered
with the memory of it after you two had put *your* stories,
black bear stories, out on the table.
Suddenly I was back in that canyon, in that gone state.
Something I hadn't thought about for years:
how I stalked a cougar that day.

So I told it. Tried to anyway,
Haines and I pretty drunk now. Wilson listening, listening,
then saying, You sure it wasn't a bobcat?
Which I secretly took as a put-down, he from the Southwest,
poet who had read that night,
and any fool able to tell a bobcat from a cougar,
even a drunk writer like me,
years later, at the smorgasbord, in California.

Hell. And then the cougar smooth-loped out of the brush
right in front of me—God, how big and beautiful he was—
jumped onto a rock and turned his head
to look at me. To look at *me!* I looked back, forgetting to shoot.
Then he jumped again, ran clear out of my life.

THE CURRENT

These fish have no eyes
these silver fish that come to me in dreams,
scattering their roe and milt
in the pockets of my brain.

But there's one that comes—
heavy, scarred, silent like the rest,
that simply holds against the current,

closing its dark mouth against
the current, closing and opening
as it holds to the current.

HUNTER

Half asleep on top of this bleak landscape,
surrounded by chukkers,
I crouch behind a pile of rocks and dream
I embrace my babysitter.
A few inches from my face
her cool and youthful eyes stare at me from two remaining
wildflowers. There's a question in those eyes
I can't answer. Who is to judge these things?
But deep under my winter underwear,
my blood stirs.

Suddenly, her hand rises in alarm—
the geese are streaming off their river island,
rising, rising up this gorge.
I move the safety. The body gathers, leans to its work.
Believe in the fingers.
Believe in the nerves.
Believe in THIS.

TRYING TO SLEEP LATE ON A
SATURDAY MORNING IN NOVEMBER

In the living room Walter Cronkite
prepares us for the moon shot.
We are approaching
the third and final phase, this
is the last exercise.
I settle down,
far down into the covers.

My son is wearing his space helmet.
I see him move down the long airless corridor,
his iron boots dragging.

My own feet grow cold.
I dream of yellow-jackets and near
frostbite, two hazards
facing the whitefish fishermen
on Satus Creek.

But there is something moving
there in the frozen reeds,
something on its side that is
slowly filling with water.
I turn onto my back.
All of me is lifting at once,
as if it were impossible to drown.

LOUISE

In the trailer next to this one
a woman picks at a child named Louise.
Didn't I tell you, Dummy, to keep this door closed?
Jesus, it's winter!
You want to pay the electric bill?
Wipe your feet, for Christ's sake!
Louise, what am I going to do with you?
Oh, what am I going to do with you, Louise?
the woman sings from morning to night.
Today the woman and child are out
hanging up wash.
Say hello to this man, the woman says
to Louise. Louise!
This is Louise, the woman says
and gives Louise a jerk.
Cat's got her tongue, the woman says.
But Louise has pins in her mouth,
wet clothes in her arms. She pulls
the line down, holds the line
with her neck
as she slings the shirt
over the line and lets go—
the shirt filling out, flapping
over her head. She ducks
and jumps back—jumps back
from this near human shape.

POEM FOR KARL WALLENDA,
AERIALIST SUPREME

When you were little, wind tailed you
all over Magdeburg. In Vienna wind looked for you
in first one courtyard then another.
It overturned fountains, it made your hair stand on end.
In Prague wind accompanied serious young couples
just starting families. But you made their breaths catch,
those ladies in long white dresses,
the men with their moustaches and high collars.
It waited in the cuffs of your sleeves
when you bowed to the Emperor Haile Selassie.
It was there when you shook hands
with the democratic King of the Belgians.
Wind rolled mangoes and garbage sacks down the streets of
        Nairobi.
You saw wind pursuing zebras across the Serengeti Plain.
Wind joined you as you stepped off the eaves of suburban houses
in Sarasota, Florida. It made little noises
in trees at every crossroads town, every circus stop.
You remarked on it all your life,
how it could come from nowhere,
how it stirred the puffy faces of the hydrangeas
below hotel room balconies while you
drew on your big Havana and watched
the smoke stream south, always south,
toward Puerto Rico and the Torrid Zone.
That morning, 74 years old and 10 stories up,
midway between hotel and hotel, a promotional stunt
on the first day of spring, that wind
which has been everywhere with you
comes in from the Caribbean to throw itself
once and for all into your arms, like a young lover!
Your hair stands on end.

You try to crouch, to reach for wire.
Later, men come along to clean up
and to take down the wire. They take down the wire
where you spent your life. Imagine that: wire.

DESCHUTES RIVER

This sky, for instance:
closed, gray,
but it has stopped snowing
so that is something. I am
so cold I cannot bend
my fingers.
Walking down to the river this morning
we surprised a badger
tearing a rabbit.
Badger had a bloody nose,
blood on its snout up to its sharp eyes:
          prowess is not to be confused
          with grace.

Later, eight mallard ducks fly over
without looking down. On the river
Frank Sandmeyer trolls, trolls
for steelhead. He has fished
this river for years
but February is the best month
he says.
Snarled, mittenless,
I handle a maze of nylon.
Far away—
another man is raising my children,
bedding my wife bedding my wife.

FOREVER

Drifting outside in a pall of smoke,
I follow a snail's streaked path down
the garden to the garden's stone wall.
Alone at last I squat on my heels, see

what needs to be done, and suddenly
affix myself to the damp stone.
I begin to look around me slowly
and listen, employing

my entire body as the snail
employs its body, relaxed, but alert.
Amazing! Tonight is a milestone
in my life. After tonight

how can I ever go back to that
other life? I keep my eyes
on the stars, wave to them
with my feelers. I hold on

for hours, just resting.
Still later, grief begins to settle
around my heart in tiny drops.
I remember my father is dead,

and I am going away from this
town soon. Forever.
Goodbye, son, my father says.
Toward morning, I climb down

and wander back into the house.
They are still waiting,
fright splashed on their faces,
as they meet my new eyes for the first time.

STORIES

DISTANCE

S he's in Milan for Christmas and wants to know what it was
like when she was a kid. Always that on the rare occasions
when he sees her.

Tell me, she says. Tell me what it was like then. She sips Strega,
waits, eyes him closely.

She is a cool, slim, attractive girl, a survivor from top to bottom.

That was a long time ago. That was twenty years ago, he says.
They're in his apartment on the Via Fabroni near the Cascina
Gardens.

You can remember, she says. Go on, tell me.

What do you want to hear? he asks. What can I tell you? I could
tell you about something that happened when you were a baby. It
involves you, he says. But only in a minor way.

Tell me, she says. But first get us another drink, so you won't
have to interrupt half way through.

He comes back from the kitchen with drinks, settles into his
chair, begins.

They were kids themselves, but they were crazy in love, this
eighteen-year-old boy and his seventeen-year-old girl friend when
they married. Not all that long afterwards they had a daughter.

The baby came along in late November during a severe cold
spell that just happened to coincide with the peak of the water-
fowl season in that part of the country. The boy loved to hunt, you
see, that's part of it.

The boy and girl, husband and wife now, father and mother,
lived in a three-room apartment under a dentist's office. Each night
they cleaned the upstairs office in exchange for their rent and
utilities. In the summer they were expected to maintain the lawn
and the flowers, and in winter the boy shoveled snow from the
walks and spread rock salt on the pavement. The two kids, I'm

113

telling you, were very much in love. On top of this they had great ambitions and they were wild dreamers. They were always talking about the things they were going to do and the places they were going to go.

He gets up from his chair and looks out the window for a minute over the tile rooftops at the snow that falls steadily through the late afternoon light.

Tell the story, she says.

The boy and girl slept in the bedroom, and the baby slept in a crib in the living room. You see, the baby was about three weeks old at this time and had only just begun to sleep through the night.

One Saturday night, after finishing his work upstairs, the boy went into the dentist's private office, put his feet up on the desk, and called Carl Sutherland, an old hunting and fishing friend of his father's.

Carl, he said when the man picked up the receiver. I'm a father. We had a baby girl.

Congratulations, boy, Carl said. How is the wife?

She's fine, Carl. The baby's fine, too, the boy said. Everybody's fine.

That's good, Carl said. I'm glad to hear it. Well, you give my regards to the wife. If you called about going hunting, I'll tell you something. The geese are flying down there to beat the band. I don't think I've ever seen so many of them and I've been going for years. I shot five today. Two this morning and three this afternoon. I'm going back in the morning and you come along if you want to.

I want to, the boy said. That's why I called.

You be here at five-thirty sharp then and we'll go, Carl said. Bring lots of shells. We'll get some shooting in all right. I'll see you in the morning.

The boy liked Carl Sutherland. He'd been a friend of the boy's father, who was dead now. After the father's death, maybe trying to replace a loss they both felt, the boy and Sutherland had started hunting together. Sutherland was a heavy-set, balding man who lived alone and was not given to casual talk. Once in a while, when they were together, the boy felt uncomfortable, wondered if he had said or done something wrong because he was not used to being around people who kept still for long periods of time. But when he did talk the older man was often opinionated, and frequently the boy didn't agree with the opinions. Yet the man had a toughness and woods-savvy about him that the boy liked and admired.

The boy hung up the telephone and went downstairs to tell the girl. She watched while he laid out his things. Hunting coat, shell bag, boots, socks, hunting cap, long underwear, pump gun.

What time will you be back? the girl asked.

Probably around noon, he said. But maybe not until after five or six o'clock. Is that too late?

It's fine, she said. We'll get along just fine. You go and have some fun. You deserve it. Maybe tomorrow evening we'll dress Catherine up and go visit Sally.

Sure, that sounds like a good idea, he said. Let's plan on that.

Sally was the girl's sister. She was ten years older. The boy was a little in love with her, just as he was a little in love with Betsy, who was another sister the girl had. He'd said to the girl, If we weren't married I could go for Sally.

What about Betsy? the girl had said. I hate to admit it but I truly feel she's better looking than Sally or me. What about her?

Betsy too, the boy said and laughed. But not in the same way I could go for Sally. There's something about Sally you could fall for. No, I believe I'd prefer Sally over Betsy, if I had to make a choice.

But who do you really love? the girl asked. Who do you love most in all the world? Who's your wife?

You're my wife, the boy said.

And will we always love each other? the girl asked, enormously enjoying this conversation he could tell.

Always, the boy said. And we'll always be together. We're like the Canada geese, he said, taking the first comparison that came to mind, for they were often on his mind in those days. They only marry once. They choose a mate early in life, and they stay together always. If one of them dies or something, the other one will never remarry. It will live off by itself somewhere, or even continue to live with the flock, but it will stay single and alone amongst all the other geese.

That's sad, the girl said. It's sadder for it to live that way, I think, alone but with all the others, than just to live off by itself somewhere.

It is sad, the boy said. But it's Nature.

Have you ever killed one of those marriages? she asked. You know what I mean.

He nodded. He said, Two or three times I've shot a goose, then a minute or two later I'd see another goose turn back from the rest and begin to circle and call over the goose that lay on the ground.

Did you shoot it too? she asked with concern.

If I could, he answered. Sometimes I missed.

And it didn't bother you? she said.

Never, he said. You can't think about it when you're doing it. You see, I love everything there is about geese. I love to just watch them even when I'm not hunting them. But there are all kinds of contradictions in life. You can't think about the contradictions.

After dinner he turned up the furnace and helped her bathe the baby. He marveled again at the infant who had half his features, the eyes and mouth, and half the girl's, the chin and the nose. He powdered the tiny body and then powdered in between the fingers and toes. He watched the girl put the baby into its diaper and pajamas.

He emptied the bath into the shower basin and then he went upstairs. It was cold and overcast outside. His breath streamed in the air. The grass, what there was of it, looked like canvas, stiff and gray under the street light. Snow lay in piles beside the walk. A car went by and he heard sand grinding under the tires. He let himself imagine what it might be like tomorrow, geese milling in the air over his head, the gun plunging against his shoulder.

Then he locked the door and went downstairs.

In bed they tried to read but both of them fell asleep, she first, letting the magazine sink to the quilt. His eyes closed, but he roused himself, checked the alarm, and turned off the lamp.

He woke to the baby's cries. The light was on out in the living room. He could see the girl standing beside the crib rocking the baby in her arms. In a minute she put the baby down, turned out the light and came back to bed.

It was two o'clock in the morning and the boy fell asleep once more.

The baby's cries woke him again. This time the girl continued to sleep. The baby cried fitfully for a few minutes and stopped. The boy listened, then began to doze.

He opened his eyes. The living room light was burning. He sat up and turned on the lamp.

I don't know what's wrong, the girl said, walking back and forth with the baby. I've changed her and given her something more to eat. But she keeps crying. She won't stop crying. I'm so tired I'm afraid I might drop her.

You come back to bed, the boy said. I'll hold her for a while.

He got up and took the baby while the girl went to lie down.

Just rock her for a few minutes, the girl said from the bedroom. Maybe she'll go back to sleep.

The boy sat on the sofa and held the baby. He jiggled it in his lap until its eyes closed. His own eyes were near closing. He rose carefully and put the baby back in the crib.

It was fifteen minutes to four and he still had forty-five minutes that he could sleep. He crawled into bed.

But a few minutes later the baby began to cry once more. This time they both got up, and the boy swore.

For God's sake what's the matter with you? the girl said to him. Maybe she's sick or something. Maybe we shouldn't have given her the bath.

The boy picked up the baby. The baby kicked its feet and was quiet. Look, the boy said, I really don't think there's anything wrong with her.

How do you know that? the girl said. Here, let me have her. I know that I ought to give her something, but I don't know what I should give her.

After a few minutes had passed and the baby had not cried, the girl put the baby down again. The boy and the girl looked at the baby, and then they looked at each other as the baby opened its eyes and began to cry.

The girl took the baby. Baby, baby, she said with tears in her eyes.

Probably it's something on her stomach, the boy said.

The girl didn't answer. She went on rocking the baby in her arms, paying no attention now to the boy.

The boy waited a minute longer then went to the kitchen and

put on water for coffee. He drew on his woolen underwear and buttoned up. Then he got into his clothes.

What are you doing? the girl said to him.

Going hunting, he said.

I don't think you should, she said. Maybe you could go later on in the day if the baby is all right then. But I don't think you should go hunting this morning. I don't want to be left alone with the baby crying like this.

Carl's planning on me going, the boy said. We've planned it.

I don't give a damn about what you and Carl have planned, she said. And I don't give a damn about Carl, either. I don't even know the man. I don't want you to go is all. I don't think you should even consider wanting to go under the circumstances.

You've met Carl before, you know him, the boy said. What do you mean you don't know him?

That's not the point and you know it, the girl said. The point is I don't intend to be left alone with a sick baby.

Wait a minute, the boy said. You don't understand.

No, you don't understand, she said. I'm your wife. This is your baby. She's sick or something. Look at her. Why is she crying? You can't leave us to go hunting.

Don't get hysterical, he said.

I'm saying you can go hunting any time, she said. Something's wrong with this baby and you want to leave us to go hunting.

She began to cry. She put the baby back in the crib, but the baby started up again. The girl dried her eyes hastily on the sleeve of her nightgown and picked the baby up once more.

The boy laced his boots slowly, put on his shirt, sweater, and his coat. The kettle whistled on the stove in the kitchen.

You're going to have to choose, the girl said. Carl or us. I mean it, you've got to choose.

What do you mean? the boy said.

You heard what I said, the girl answered. If you want a family you're going to have to choose.

They stared at each other. Then the boy took his hunting gear and went upstairs. He started the car, went around to the windows and, making a job of it, scraped away the ice.

The temperature had dropped during the night, but the weather had cleared so that stars had come out. The stars gleamed in the sky over his head. Driving, the boy looked out at the stars and was moved when he considered their distance.

Carl's porchlight was on, his station wagon parked in the drive with the motor idling. Carl came outside as the boy pulled to the curb. The boy had decided.

You might want to park off the street, Carl said as the boy came up the walk. I'm ready, just let me hit the lights. I feel like hell, I really do, he went on. I thought maybe you had overslept so I just this minute called your place. Your wife said you had left. I feel like hell.

It's okay, the boy said, trying to pick his words. He leaned his weight on one leg and turned up his collar. He put his hands in his coat pockets. She was already up, Carl. We've both been up for a while. I guess there's something wrong with the baby. I don't know. The baby keeps crying, I mean. The thing is, I guess I can't go this time, Carl.

You should have just stepped to the phone and called me, boy, Carl said. It's okay. You know you didn't have to come over here to tell me. What the hell, this hunting business you can take it or leave it. It's not important. You want a cup of coffee?

I'd better get back, the boy said.

Well, I expect I'll go ahead then, Carl said. He looked at the boy. The boy kept standing on the porch, not saying anything.

It's cleared up, Carl said. I don't look for much action this morning. Probably you won't have missed anything anyway.

The boy nodded. I'll see you, Carl, he said.

So long, Carl said. Hey, don't let anybody ever tell you otherwise, Carl said. You're a lucky boy and I mean that.

The boy started his car and waited. He watched Carl go through the house and turn off all the lights. Then the boy put the car in gear and pulled away from the curb.

The living room light was on, but the girl was asleep on the bed and the baby was asleep beside her.

The boy took off his boots, pants and shirt. He was quiet about it. In his socks and woolen underwear, he sat on the sofa and read the morning paper.

Soon it began to turn light outside. The girl and the baby slept on. After a while the boy went to the kitchen and began to fry bacon.

The girl came out in her robe a few minutes later and put her arms around him without saying anything.

Hey, don't catch your robe on fire, the boy said. She was leaning against him but touching the stove, too.

I'm sorry about earlier, she said. I don't know what got into me. I don't know why I said those things.

It's all right, he said. Here, let me get this bacon.

I didn't mean to snap like that, she said. It was awful.

It was my fault, he said. How's Catherine?

She's fine now. I don't know what was the matter with her earlier. I changed her again after you left, and then she was fine. She was just fine and she went right off to sleep. I don't know what it was. Don't be mad with us.

The boy laughed. I'm not mad with you. Don't be silly, he said. Here, let me do something with this pan.

You sit down, the girl said. I'll fix this breakfast. How does a waffle sound with this bacon?

Sounds great, he said. I'm starved.

She took the bacon out of the pan and then she made waffle batter. He sat at the table, relaxed now, and watched her move around the kitchen.

She left to close their bedroom door. In the living room she put on a record that they both liked.

We don't want to wake that one up again, the girl said.

That's for sure, the boy said and laughed.

She put a plate in front of him with bacon, a fried egg, and a waffle. She put another plate on the table for herself. It's ready, she said.

It looks swell, he said. He spread butter and poured syrup over the waffle. But as he started to cut into the waffle, he turned the plate into his lap.

I don't believe it, he said, jumping up from the table.

The girl looked at him and then at the expression on his face. She began to laugh.

If you could see yourself in the mirror, she said. She kept laughing.

He looked down at the syrup that covered the front of his woolen underwear, at the pieces of waffle, bacon, and egg that clung to the syrup. He began to laugh.

I was starved, he said, shaking his head.

You were starved, she said, laughing.

He peeled off the woolen underwear and threw it at the bathroom door. Then he opened his arms and she moved into them.

We won't fight any more, she said. It's not worth it, is it?

That's right, he said.

We won't fight any more, she said.

The boy said, We won't. Then he kissed her.

He gets up from his chair and refills their glasses.

That's it, he says. End of story. I admit it's not much of one.

I was interested, she says. It was very interesting if you want to know. But what happened? she says. I mean later.

He shrugs and carries his drink over to the window. It's dark now but still snowing.

Things change, he says. I don't know how they do. But they do without your realizing it or wanting them to.

Yes, that's true, only—but she does not finish what she started.

She drops the subject then. In the window's reflection he sees her study her nails. Then she raises her head. Speaking brightly, she asks if he is going to show her the city, after all.

He says, Put your boots on and let's go.

But he stays by the window, remembering that life. They had laughed. They had leaned on each other and laughed until the tears had come, while everything else—the cold and where he'd go in it—was outside, for a while anyway.

THE LIE

It's a lie," my wife said. "How could you believe such a thing? She's jealous, that's all." She tossed her head and kept staring at me. She hadn't yet taken off her hat and coat. Her face was flushed from the accusation. "You believe me, don't you? Surely you don't believe that?"

I shrugged. Then I said, "Why should she lie? Where would it get her? What would she have to gain by lying?" I was uncomfortable. I stood there in my slippers opening and closing my hands, feeling a little ridiculous and on display in spite of the circumstances. I'm not cut out to play the inquisitor. I wish now it had never reached my ears, that everything could have been as before. "She's supposed to be a friend," I said. "A friend to both of us."

"She's a bitch, is what she is! You don't think a friend, however poor a friend, even a chance acquaintance, would tell a thing like that, such an outright lie, do you? You simply can't believe it." She shook her head at my folly. Then she unpinned her hat, pulled off her gloves, laid everything on the table. She removed her coat and dropped it over the back of a chair.

"I don't know what to believe any more," I said. "I want to believe you."

"Then do!" she said. "Believe me—that's all I'm asking. I'm telling you the truth. I wouldn't lie about something like that. There now. Say it isn't true, darling. Say you don't believe it."

I love her. I wanted to take her in my arms, hold her, tell her I believed her. But the lie, if it was a lie, had come between us. I moved over to the window.

"You must believe me," she said. "You know this is stupid. You know I'm telling you the truth."

I stood at the window and looked down at the traffic moving slowly below. If I raised my eyes, I could see my wife's reflection in the window. I'm a broad-minded man, I told myself. I can work this through. I began to think about my wife, about our life together, about truth versus fiction, honesty opposed to falsehood, illusion and reality. I thought about that movie *Blow-up* we'd recently seen. I remembered the biography of Leo Tolstoy that lay on the coffee table, the things he says about truth, the splash he'd made in old Russia. Then I recalled a friend from long ago, a friend I'd had in my junior and senior years of high school. A friend who could never tell the truth, a chronic, unmitigated liar, yet a pleasant, well-meaning person and a true friend for two or three years during a difficult period in my life. I was overjoyed with my discovery of this habitual liar from out of my past, this precedent to draw upon for aid in the present crisis in our—up to now—happy marriage. This person, this spirited liar, could indeed bear out my wife's theory that there were such people in the world. I was happy again. I turned around to speak. I knew what I wanted to say: Yes, indeed, it could be true, it *is* true—people can and do lie, uncontrollably, perhaps unconsciously, pathologically at times, without thought to the consequences. Surely my informant was such a person. But just at that moment my wife sat down on the sofa, covered her face with her hands and said, "It's true, God forgive me. Everything she told you is true. It was a lie when I said I didn't know anything about it."

"Is that true?" I said. I sat down in one of the chairs near the window.

She nodded. She kept her hands over her face.

I said, "Why did you deny it, then? We never lie to one another. Haven't we always told each other the truth?"

"I was sorry," she said. She looked at me and shook her head. "I was ashamed. You don't know how ashamed I was. I didn't want you to believe it."

"I think I understand," I said.

She kicked off her shoes and leaned back on the sofa. Then she sat up and tugged her sweater over her head. She patted her hair into place. She took one of the cigarettes from the tray. I held the lighter for her and was momentarily astonished by the sight of her slim, pale fingers and her well-manicured nails. It was as if I were seeing them in a new and somehow revealing way.

She drew on the cigarette and said, after a minute, "And how was your day today, sweet? Generally speaking, that is. You know what I mean." She held the cigarette between her lips and stood up for a minute to step out of her skirt. "There," she said.

"It was so-so," I answered. "There was a policeman here in the afternoon, with a warrant, believe it or not, looking for someone who used to live down the hall. And the apartment manager himself called to say the water would be shut off for a half-hour between three and three-thirty while they made repairs. In fact, come to think of it, it was just during the time the policeman was here that they had to shut off the water."

"Is that so?" she said. She put her hands on her hips and stretched. Then she closed her eyes, yawned, and shook her long hair.

"And I read a good portion of the Tolstoy book today," I said.

"Marvelous." She began to eat cocktail nuts, tossing them one after the other with her right hand into her open mouth, while still holding the cigarette between the fingers of her left hand. From time to time she stopped eating long enough to wipe her lips with the back of her hand and draw on the cigarette. She'd slipped out of her underthings by now. She doubled her legs under her and settled into the sofa. "How is it?" she said.

"He had some interesting ideas," I said. "He was quite a character." My fingers tingled and the blood was beginning to move faster. But I felt weak, too.

"Come here my little muzhik," she said.

"I want the truth," I said faintly, on my hands and knees now. The plush, springy softness of the carpet excited me. Slowly I crawled over to the sofa and rested my chin on one of the cushions. She ran her hand through my hair. She was still smiling. Grains of salt glimmered on her full lips. But as I watched, her eyes filled with a look of inexpressible sadness, though she continued smiling and stroking my hair.

"Little Pasha," she said. "Come up here, dumpling. Did it really believe that nasty lady, that nasty lie? Here, put your head on mommy's breast. That's it. Now close your eyes. There. How could it believe such a thing? I'm disappointed in you. Really, you know me better than that. Lying is just a sport for some people."

THE CABIN

Mr. Harrold came out of the cafe to find it'd stopped snowing. The sky was clearing behind the hills on the other side of the river. He stopped beside the car for a minute and stretched, holding the car door open while he drew a big mouthful of cold air. He'd swear he could almost taste this air. He eased in behind the steering wheel and got back on the highway. It was only an hour's drive to the lodge. He could get in a couple of hours of fishing this afternoon. Then there was tomorrow. All day tomorrow.

At Parke Junction he took the bridge over the river and turned off onto the road that would take him to the lodge. Pine trees whose branches were heavy with snow stood on either side of the road. Clouds mantled the white hills so that it was hard to tell where the hills ended and the sky began. It reminded him of those Chinese landscapes they'd looked at that time in the museum in Portland. He liked them. He'd said as much to Frances, but she didn't say anything back. She'd spent a few minutes with him in that wing of the gallery and then moved on to the next exhibit.

It was going on noon when he reached the lodge. He saw the cabins up on the hill and then, as the road straightened out, the lodge itself. He slowed, bumped off the road onto the dirty, sand-covered parking lot, and stopped the car up close to the front door. He rolled down the window and rested for a minute, working his shoulders back and forth into the seat. He closed and then opened his eyes. A flickering neon sign said Castlerock and below that, on a neat, hand-painted sign, Deluxe Cabins—OFFICE. The last time he'd been here—Frances had been with him that time—they'd stayed for four days, and he'd landed five nice fish downriver. That had been three years ago. They used to come here often, two or three times a year. He opened the door and got out of the car slowly, feeling the stiffness in his back and neck. He walked heavily across the frozen snow and stuck his hands in his coat pockets as he started up the planked steps. At the top he scraped the snow and grit off his shoes and nodded to a young couple coming out. He noticed the way the man held the woman's arm as they went down the steps.

Inside the lodge there was the smell of wood smoke and fried ham. He heard the clatter of dishes. He looked at the big Brown trout mounted over the fireplace in the dining room, and he felt glad to be back. Near the cash register, where he stood, was a display case with leather purses, wallets, and pairs of moccasins arranged behind the glass. Scattered around on top of the case were Indian bead necklaces and bracelets and pieces of petrified wood. He moved over to the horseshoe-shaped counter and took a stool. Two men sitting a few stools down stopped talking and turned their heads to look at him. They were hunters, and their red hats and coats lay on an empty table behind them. Mr. Harrold waited and pulled at his fingers.

"How long you been here?" the girl asked, frowning. She'd come on him soundlessly, from the kitchen. She put down a glass of water in front of him.

"Not long," Mr. Harrold said.

"You should've rung the bell," she said. Her braces glittered as she opened and closed her mouth.

"I'm supposed to have a cabin," he said. "I wrote you a card and made a reservation a week or so ago."

"I'll have to get Mrs. Maye," the girl said. "She's cooking. She's the one who looks after the cabins. She didn't say anything to me about it. We don't usually keep them open in the winter, you know."

"I wrote you a card," he said. "You check with Mrs. Maye. You ask her about it." The two men had turned on their stools to look at him again.

"I'll get Mrs. Maye," the girl said.

Flushed, he closed his hands together on the counter in front of him. A big Frederic Remington reproduction hung on the wall at the far end of the room. He watched the lurching, frightened buffalo, and the Indians with the drawn bows fixed at their shoulders.

"Mr. Harrold!" the old woman called, hobbling toward him. She was a small gray-haired woman with heavy breasts and a fat throat. The straps to her underwear showed through her white uniform. She undid her apron and held out her hand.

"Glad to see you, Mrs. Maye," he said as he got up off the stool.

"I hardly recognized you," the old woman said. "I don't know what's the matter with the girl sometimes...Edith...she's my granddaughter. My daughter and her husband are looking after the place now." She took her glasses off and began wiping away the steam from the lenses.

He looked down at the polished counter. He smoothed his fingers over the grainy wood.

"Where's the Missus?" she asked.

"She didn't feel too well this week," Mr. Harrold said. He started to say something else, but there was nothing else to say.

"I'm sorry to hear that! I had the cabin fixed up nice for the two of you," Mrs. Maye said. She took off the apron and put it behind the cash register. "Edith! I'm taking Mr. Harrold to his cabin! I'll have to get my coat, Mr. Harrold." The girl didn't answer. But she came to the kitchen door with a coffee pot in her hand and stared at them.

Outside the sun had come out and the glare hurt his eyes. He held onto the banister and went slowly down the stairs, following Mrs. Maye, who limped.

"Sun's bad, isn't it?" she said, moving carefully over the packed snow. He felt she ought to be using a cane. "The first time it's been out all week," she said. She waved at some people going by in a car.

They went past a gasoline pump, locked and covered with snow, and past a little shed with a TIRES sign hung over the door. He looked through the broken windows at the heaps of burlap sacks inside, the old tires, and the barrels. The room was damp and cold-looking. Snow had drifted inside and lay sprinkled on the sill around the broken glass.

"Kids have done that," Mrs. Maye said, stopping for a minute and putting her hand up to the broken window. "They don't miss a chance to do us dirt. A whole pack of them are all the time running wild from down at the construction camp." She shook her head. "Poor little devils. Sorry home life for kids anyway, always on the move like that. Their daddies are building on that dam." She unlocked the cabin door and pushed on it. "I laid a little fire this morning so it would be nice for you," she said.

"I appreciate that, Mrs. Maye," he said.

There was a big double bed covered with a plain bedspread, a bureau, and a desk in the front room which was divided from the kitchen by a little plywood partition. There was also a sink, wood stove, woodbox, an old ice-box, an oilcloth covered table and two wooden chairs. A door opened to a bathroom. He saw a little porch to one side where he could hang his clothes.

"Looks fine," he said.

"I tried to make it as nice as I could," she said. "Do you need anything now, Mr. Harrold?"

"Not now anyway, thanks," he said.

"I'll let you rest then. You're probably tired, driving all that way," she said.

"I should bring in my things," Mr. Harrold said, following her out. He shut the door behind them and they stood on the porch looking down the hill.

"I'm just sorry your wife couldn't come," the old woman said.

He didn't answer.

From where they stood they were almost on a level with the huge rock protruding from the hillside behind the road. Some people said it looked like a petrified castle. "How's the fishing?" he said.

"Some of them are getting fish, but most of the men are out hunting," she said. "Deer season, you know."

He drove the car as close as he could to the cabin and started to unload. The last thing he took out of the car was a pint of Scotch from the glove compartment. He set the bottle on the table. Later, as he spread out the boxes of weights and hooks and thick-bodied red and white flies, he moved the bottle to the drainboard. Sitting there at the table smoking a cigarette with his tackle box open and everything in its place, his flies and the weights spread out, testing leader strength between his hands and tying up outfits for that afternoon, he was glad he'd come after all. And he'd still be able to get in a couple of hours fishing this afternoon. Then there was tomorrow. He'd already decided he would save some of the bottle for when he came back from fishing that afternoon and have the rest for tomorrow.

As he sat at the table tying up outfits, he thought he heard something digging out on the porch. He got up from the table and opened the door. But there was nothing there. There were only the white hills and the dead-looking pines under the overcast sky and, down below, the few buildings and some cars drawn up beside the highway. He was all at once very tired and thought he would lie down on the bed for a few minutes. He didn't want to sleep. He'd just lie down and rest, and then he'd get up, dress, take his things, and walk down to the river. He cleaned off the table, undressed, and then got in between the cold sheets. For a while he lay on his side, eyes closed, knees drawn up for warmth, then he turned onto his back and wiggled his toes against the sheet. He wished Frances were here. He wished there were somebody to talk to.

He opened his eyes. The room was dark. The stove gave off little crackling noises, and there was a red glow on the wall behind the stove. He lay in bed and stared at the window, not able to believe it was really dark outside. He shut his eyes again and then opened them. He'd only wanted to rest. He hadn't intended to fall asleep. He opened his eyes and sat up heavily on the side of the bed. He got on his shirt and reached for his pants. He went into the bathroom and threw water on his face.

"Goddamn it!" he said, banging things around in the kitchen cupboard, taking down some cans and putting them back again. He made a pot of coffee and drank two cups before deciding to go down to the cafe for something to eat. He put on wool slippers and a coat and hunted around until he found his flashlight. Then he went outside.

The cold air stung his cheeks and pinched his nostrils together. But the air felt good to him. It cleared his head. The lights from the lodge showed him where he was walking, and he was careful. Inside the cafe, he nodded to the girl, Edith, and sat down in a booth near the end of the counter. He could hear a radio playing back in the kitchen. The girl made no effort to wait on him.

"Are you closed?" Mr. Harrold said.

"Kind of. I'm cleaning up for the morning," she said.

"Too late for something to eat then," he said.

"I guess I can get you something," she said. She came over with a menu.

"Mrs. Maye around, Edith?"

"She's up in her room. Did you need her for something?"

"I need more wood. For in the morning."

"It's out in back," she said. "Right here behind the kitchen."

He pointed to something simple on the menu—a ham sandwich with potato salad. "I'll have this," he said.

As he waited, he began moving the salt and pepper shakers around in a little circle in front of him. After she brought his plate to him, she hung around out in front, filling sugar bowls and napkin holders, looking up at him from time to time. Pretty soon, before he'd finished, she came over with a wet rag and began wiping off his table.

He left some money, considerably more than the bill, and went out through a door at the side of the lodge. He went around back where he picked up an armload of wood. Then the snail's pace climb up to the cabin. He looked back once and saw the girl watching him from the kitchen window. By the time he got to his door and dropped the wood, he hated her.

He lay on the bed for a long time and read old *Life* magazines that he'd found on the porch. When the heat from the fire finally made him sleepy, he got up and cleared off his bed, then arranged his things for the next morning. He looked through the pile of stuff again to make sure he had everything. He liked things in order and didn't want to get up the next morning and have to look for something. He picked up the Scotch and held the bottle up to the light. Then he poured some into a cup. He carried the cup over to the bed and set it on the nightstand. He turned off the light and stood looking out the window for a minute before getting into bed.

He got up so early it was still almost dark in the cabin. The fire had gone down to coals during the night. He could see his breath in the cabin. He adjusted the grate and pushed in some wood. He couldn't remember the last time he'd gotten up so early. He fixed peanut butter sandwiches and wrapped them in waxed paper. He put the sandwiches and some oatmeal cookies into a coat pocket. At the door he pulled on his waders.

The light outside was vague and gray. Clouds filled the long valleys and hung in patches over the trees and mountains. The lodge was dark. He moved out slowly down the packed, slippery trail toward the river. It pleased him to be up this early and to be going fishing. Somewhere in one of the valleys off behind the river he heard the pop-pop of shots and counted them. Seven. Eight. The hunters were awake. And the deer. He wondered if the shots came from the two hunters he'd seen in the lodge yesterday. Deer didn't have much of a chance in snow like this. He kept his eyes down, watching the trail. It kept dropping downhill and soon he was in heavy timber with snow up to his ankles.

Snow lay in drifts under the trees, but it wasn't too deep where he walked. It was a good trail, packed solid, thick with pine needles that crunched into the snow under his boots. He could see his breath streaming out in front of him. He held the fishing rod straight ahead of him when he had to push through the bushes or go under trees with low limbs. He held the rod by its big reel, tucked up under his arm like a lance. Sometimes, back when he was a kid and had gone into a remote area to fish for two or three days at a time, hiking in by himself, he'd carried his rod like this, even when there was no brush or trees, maybe just a big green meadow. Those times he would imagine himself waiting for his opponent to ride out of the trees on a horse. The jays at the crowded edge of the woods would scream. Then he'd sing something as loud as he could. Yell defiance until his chest hurt, at the hawks that circled and circled over the meadow. The sun and the sky came back to him now, and the lake with the lean-to. The water so clear and green you could see fifteen or twenty feet down to where it shelved off into deeper water. He could hear the river. But the trail was gone now and just before he started down the bank to the river, he stepped into a snowdrift up over his knees and panicked, clawing up handfuls of snow and vines to get out.

The river looked impossibly cold. It was silver-green in color and there was ice on the little pools in the rocks along the edge. Before, in the summer, he'd caught his fish further downriver. But he couldn't go downriver this morning. This morning he was simply glad to be where he was. A hundred feet away, on the other side of the river, lay a beach with a nice riffle running just in front of the beach. But of course there was no way of getting over there. He decided he was just fine where he was. He lifted up onto a log, positioned himself there, and looked around. He saw tall trees and snow-covered mountains. He thought it was pretty as a picture, the way the steam lay over the river. He sat there on the log swinging his legs back and forth while he threaded the line through the guides of his rod. He tied on one of the outfits he'd made up last night. When everything was ready he slipped down off the log, pulled the rubber boots up over his legs as high as they'd go, and fastened the buckle tops of the waders to his belt. He waded slowly into the river, holding his breath for the cold water shock. The water hit and, swirling, braced against him up to his knees. He stopped, then he moved out a little further. He took the brake off his reel and made a nice cast upstream.

As he fished, he began to feel some of the old excitement coming back. He kept on fishing. After a time he waded out and sat down on a rock with his back against a log. He took out the cookies. He wasn't going to hurry anything. Not today. A flock of small birds flew from across the river and perched on some rocks close to where he was sitting. They rose when he scattered a handful of crumbs toward them. The tops of the trees creaked and the wind was drawing the clouds up out of the valley and over the hills. Then he heard a spatter of shots from somewhere in the forest across the river.

He'd just changed flies and made his cast when he saw the deer. It stumbled out of the brush upriver and ran onto the little beach, shaking and twisting its head, ropes of white mucous hanging from its nostrils. Its left hind leg was broken and dragged behind as, for an instant, the deer stopped, and turned her head back to look at it. Then she went into the river and out into the current until only her back and head were visible. She reached the shallow water on his side and came out clumsily, moving her head from side to side. He stood very still and watched her plunge into the trees.

"Dirty bastards," he said.

He made another cast. Then he reeled in and made his way back to the shore. He sat down in the same place on the log and ate his sandwich. It was dry and it didn't have any taste to it, but he ate it anyway and tried not to think about the deer. Frances would be up now, doing things around the house. He didn't want to think about Frances, either. But he remembered that morning when he'd caught the three steelhead. It was all he could do to carry them up the hill to their cabin. But he had, and when she came to the door, he'd emptied them out of the sack onto the steps in front of her. She'd whistled and bent down to touch the black spots that ran along their backs. And he'd gone back that afternoon and caught two more.

It had turned colder. The wind was blowing down the river. He got up stiffly and hobbled over the rocks trying to loosen up. He thought about building a fire, but then decided he wouldn't stay much longer. Some crows flapped by overhead coming from across the river. When they were over him he yelled, but they didn't even look down.

He changed flies again, added more weight and cast upstream. He let the current draw the line through his fingers until he saw it go slack. Then he set the brake on his reel. The pencil-lead weight bounced against the rocks under the water. He held the butt of the rod against his stomach and wondered how the fly might look to a fish.

Several boys came out of the trees upriver and walked onto the beach. Some of them were wearing red hats and down vests. They moved around on the beach, looking at Mr. Harrold and then looking up and down the river. When they began moving down the beach in his direction, Mr. Harrold looked up at the hills, then downriver to where the best water was. He began to reel in. He caught his fly and set the hook into the cork above the reel. Then he started easing his way back toward the shore, thinking only of the shore and that each careful step brought him one step closer.

"Hey!"

He stopped and turned slowly around in the water, wishing this thing had happened when he was on the shore and not out here with the water pushing against his legs and him off balance on the slippery rocks. His feet wedged themselves down between rocks while he kept his eyes on them until he'd picked out the leader. All of them wore what looked like holsters or knife sheaths on their belts. But only one boy had a rifle. It was, he knew, the boy who'd called to him. Gaunt and thin-faced, wearing a brown duck-billed cap, the boy said:

"You see a deer come out up there?" The boy held the gun in his right hand, as if it were a pistol, and pointed the barrel up the beach.

One of the boys said, "Sure he did, Earl, it ain't been very long," and looked around at the four others. They nodded. They passed round a cigarette and kept their eyes on him.

"I said—Hey you deaf? I said did you see him?"

"It wasn't a him, it was a her," Mr. Harrold said. "And her back leg was almost shot off, for Christ's sake."

"What's that to you?" the one with the gun said.

"He's pretty smart, ain't he, Earl? Tell us where it went, you old son of a bitch!" one of the boys said.

"Where'd he go?" the boy asked, and raised the gun to his hip, half pointing it across at Mr. Harrold.

"Who wants to know?" He held the rod straight ahead, tight up under his arm and with his other hand he pulled down his hat. "You little bastards are from that trailer camp up the river, aren't you?"

"You think you know a lot, don't you?" the boy said, looking around him at the others, nodding at them. He raised up one foot and set it down slowly, then the other. In a moment, he raised the rifle to his shoulder and pulled back the hammer.

The barrel was pointed at Mr. Harrold's stomach, or else a little lower down. The water swirled and foamed around his boots. He opened and closed his mouth. But he was not able to move his tongue. He looked down into the clear water at the rocks and the little spaces of sand. He wondered what it would be like if his boots tipped water and he went down, rolling like a chunk.

"What's the matter with you?" he asked the boy. The ice water came up through his legs then and poured into his chest.

The boy didn't say anything. He just stood there. All of them just stood there looking at him.

"Don't shoot," Mr. Harrold said.

The boy held the gun on him for another minute, then he lowered it. "Scared, wasn't you?"

Mr. Harrold nodded his head dreamily. He felt as if he wanted to yawn. He kept opening and closing his mouth.

One of the boys pried loose a rock from the edge of the water and threw it. Mr. Harrold turned his back and the rock hit the water two feet away from him. The others began throwing. He stood there looking at the shore, hearing the rocks splash around him.

"You didn't want to fish here anyway, did you?" the boy said. "I could've got you, but I didn't. You see that deer, you remember how lucky you was."

Mr. Harrold stood there a minute longer. Then he looked over his shoulder. One of the boys gave him the finger, and the rest of them grinned. Then they moved together back into the trees. He watched them go. He turned and worked his way back to the shore and dropped down against the log. After a few minutes he got up and started the walk back to the cabin.

The snow had held back all morning and now, just as he was in sight of the clearing, light flakes began falling. His rod was back there somewhere. Maybe he'd left it when he stopped that one time after he turned his ankle. He could remember laying the rod on the snow as he tried to undo his boot, but he didn't recall picking it up. Anyway, it didn't matter to him now. It was a good rod and one that he'd paid over ninety dollars for one summer five or six years ago. But even if it were nice tomorrow, he wouldn't go back for it. Tomorrow? He had to be back home and at work tomorrow. A jay cried from a nearby tree, and another answered from across the clearing by his cabin. He was tired and walking slowly by now, trying to keep weight off his foot.

He came out of the trees and stopped. Lights were on down at the lodge. Even the lights in the parking area were on. There were still many hours of daylight left, but they had turned on all the lights down there. This seemed mysterious and impenetrable to him. Had something happened? He shook his head. Then he went up the steps to his cabin. He stopped on the porch. He didn't want to go inside. But he understood he had to open the door and enter the room. He didn't know if he could do that. He thought for a minute of just getting into his car and driving away. He looked once more down the hill at the lights. Then he grasped the door knob and opened the door to his cabin.

Someone, Mrs. Maye, he supposed, had built a little fire in the stove. Still, he looked around cautiously. It was quiet, except for the sizzling of the fire. He sat down on the bed and began to work off his boots. Then he sat there in his stocking feet, thinking of the river and of the large fish that must even now be moving upriver in that heart-stopping cold water. He shook his head, got up, and held his hands a few inches from the stove, opening and closing his fingers until they tingled. He let the warmth gradually come back into his body. He began to think of home, of getting back there before dark.

HARRY'S DEATH

Mazatlan, Mexico—three months later

Everything has changed since Harry's death. Being down here, for instance. Who'd have thought it, only three short months ago, that I'd be down here in Mexico and poor Harry dead and buried? Harry! Dead and buried—but not forgotten.

I couldn't go to work that day when I got the news. I was just too torn up. Jack Berger, who is the fender-and-body man at Frank's Custom Repair where we all work, called me at 6:30 a.m. as I was having a cup of coffee and a cigarette before sitting down to breakfast.

"Harry's dead," he said just like that, dropping the bomb. "Turn on your radio," he said. "Turn on your TV."

The police had just left his house after asking Jack a lot of questions about Harry. They'd told him to come down right away and identify the body. Jack said they'd probably come to my place next. Why they went to Jack Berger's place first is a mystery to me since he and Harry weren't what you'd say close. Not as close anyway as Harry and me.

I couldn't believe it, but I knew it must be true for Jack to call. I felt like I was in shock and forgot all about breakfast. I turned from one news broadcast to another until I had the story. I must have hung around an hour or so listening to the radio and getting more and more upset as I thought about Harry and what the radio was saying. There would be a lot of crummy people who wouldn't be sorry to see Harry dead, would be glad he'd bought it in fact. His wife for one would be glad, though she lived in San Diego and they hadn't seen each other for two or three years. She'd be glad. She's that kind of person, from what Harry had said. She didn't want to give him the divorce for another woman. No divorce, nothing. Now she wouldn't have to worry about it any more. No, she wouldn't be sorry to see Harry dead. But Little Judith, that's another story.

I left the house after calling in at work to report off. Frank didn't say much, he said he could understand. He felt the same way, he said, but he had to keep the shop open. Harry would have wanted it that way, he said. Frank Klovee. He's the owner and shop foreman rolled into one, and the best man I ever worked for.

I got in the car and started off in the general direction of the Red Fox, a place where Harry and myself and Gene Smith and Rod Williams and Ned Clark and some of the rest of the gang hung out nights after work. It was 8:30 in the morning by then and the traffic was heavy, so I had to keep my mind on my driving. Still, I couldn't help thinking now and then about poor Harry.

Harry was an operator. That is to say he always had something going. It was never a drag being around Harry. He was good with women, if you know what I mean, always had money and lived high. He was sharp too and somehow he could always work it around so that in any deal he came out smelling like a rose. The Jag he drove, for instance. It was nearly new, a twenty-thousand-dollar car, but it had been wrecked in a big pileup on 101. Harry bought it for a song from the insurance company and fixed it up himself till it was like new. That's the kind of guy Harry was. Then there's this thirty-two-foot Chris Craft cabin cruiser that Harry's uncle in L.A. had left Harry in his will. Harry'd only had the boat about a month. He'd just gone down to look it over and take it out for a little spin a couple of weeks ago. But there was the problem of Harry's wife who was legally entitled to her share. To keep her from somehow getting her hands on it if she got wind of it—before he'd even laid eyes on the boat in fact—Harry had gone to a lawyer and worked something out so that he signed the thing over lock, stock, and pickle barrel to Little Judith. The two of them had been planning to take it for a trip someplace on Harry's vacation in August. Harry had been all over, I might add. He'd been to Europe when he was in the service and had been to all the capitals and big resort cities. He'd been in a crowd once when someone took a shot at General de Gaulle. He'd been places and done things, Harry had. Now he was dead.

At the Red Fox, which opens early, there was only one guy in the place. He was sitting at the other end of the bar, and he was no one I knew. Jimmy, the bartender, had the television on and nodded at me as I came in. His eyes were red and it came home to me hard, Harry's death, when I saw Jimmy. There was an old Lucille Ball-Desi Arnaz show just starting and Jimmy took a long stick and turned the channel selector to another station, but there was nothing on right now about Harry.

"I can't believe it," Jimmy said, shaking his head. "Anybody but Harry."

"I feel the same way, Jimmy," I said. "Anybody but Harry."

Jimmy poured us two stiff ones and threw his off without batting an eye. "It hurts as bad as if Harry'd been my own brother. It couldn't hurt any worse." He shook his head again and stared a while at his glass. He was pretty far gone already.

"We'd better have another one," he said.

"Put a little water in mine this time," I said.

A few guys, friends of Harry's, drifted in from time to time that morning. Once I saw Jimmy get out a handkerchief and blow his nose. The guy at the other end of the bar, the stranger, made a move as if to play something on the juke box. But Jimmy went over and pulled the plug with a wild jerk and glared at the guy till he left. None of us had much to say to each other. What could we say? We were still too numb. Finally Jimmy brought out an empty cigar box and put it on the bar. He said we'd better start a collection for a wreath. We all put in a dollar or two to get things going. Jimmy took a grease pencil and marked HARRY FUND on the box.

Mike Demarest came in and took the stool next to mine. He's a bartender at the T-'N-T Club. "Cripes!" he said. "I heard it on the clock radio. The wife was getting dressed for work and woke me up and said, 'Is that the Harry you know?' Sure as hell. Give me a double and a beer chaser, Jimmy."

In a few minutes he said, "How's Little Judith taking it? Has anybody seen Little Judith?" I could see he was watching me out of the corner of his eye. I didn't have anything to say to him. Jimmy said, "She called here this morning and sounded pretty hysterical, poor kid."

After another drink or two, Mike turned to me and said, "You going down to view him?"

I waited for a minute before answering. "I don't care much for that sort of thing. I doubt it."

Mike nodded as if he understood. But a minute later I caught him watching me in the mirror behind the bar. I might put in here that I don't like Mike Demarest, if you haven't already guessed. I have never liked him. Harry didn't like him either. We'd talked about it. But that's the way it always is—the good guys get it and the others go about their business.

About then I noticed my palms were getting clammy and my insides felt like lead. At the same time I could feel the blood pounding hard in my temples. For a minute I thought I was going to faint. I slid off the stool, nodded at Mike and said, "Take it easy, Jimmy."

"Yeah, you too," he said.

Outside I leaned against the wall for a minute, trying to get my bearings. I remembered I hadn't had any breakfast. What with the anxiety and depression and the drinks I'd had, it was no wonder my head was spinning. But I didn't want anything to eat. I couldn't have eaten a bite for anything. A clock over a jewelry store window across the street said ten to eleven. It seemed like it should be late afternoon at least, so much had happened.

It was at that moment I saw Little Judith. She came around the corner walking slowly, her shoulders hunched and drawn, a pinched look to her face. A pitiful sight. She had a big wad of Kleenex in her hand. She stopped once and blew her nose.

"Judith," I said.

She made a sound that went to my heart like a bullet. We put our arms around each other right there on the sidewalk.

I said, "Judith, I'm so sorry. What can I do? I'd give my right arm, you know that."

She nodded. She couldn't say anything. We stood there patting and rubbing each other, me trying to console her, saying whatever came to mind, both of us sniffling. She let go for a minute and looked at me with a dazed look, then she threw her arms around me again.

"I can't, I can't believe it, that's all," she said. "I just can't." She kept squeezing my shoulder with one hand and patting my back with the other.

"It's true, Judith," I said. "It's on the radio and TV news, and it'll be in all the papers tonight."

"No, no," she said, squeezing me all the harder.

I was beginning to get woozy again. I could feel the sun burning down on my head. She still had her arms around me. I moved just enough so that we had to pull apart. But I kept my arm around her waist to give her support.

"We were going away next month," she said. "Last night we sat at our table in the Red Fox for three or four hours, making plans."

"Judith," I said, "let's go someplace and have a cup of coffee or a drink."

"Let's go inside," she said.

"No, someplace else," I said. "We can come back here later."

"I think if I ate something I might feel better," she said.

"That's a good idea," I said. "I could eat something."

The next three days passed in a whirl. I went to work each day, but it was a sad and depressing place without Harry. I saw a lot of Little Judith after work. I sat with her in the evenings and tried to keep her from dwelling on too many unpleasant aspects of the thing. I also took her around here and there for things she had to attend to. Twice I took her to the funeral parlor. She collapsed the first time. I wouldn't go inside the place myself. I wanted to remember poor Harry as he used to be.

The day before the service all of us at the shop chipped in thirty-eight bucks for a funeral spray. I was delegated to go and pick it out since I'd been close to Harry. I remembered a florist's not too far from my place. So I drove home, fixed some lunch, then drove to Howard's House of Flowers. It was in this shopping center along with a pharmacy, a barber shop, a bank and a travel agency. I parked the car and hadn't taken more than a couple of steps when my eye was caught by this big poster in the travel agency window. I went over to the window and stood for a while. Mexico. There was this giant stone face grinning down like the sun over a blue sea filled with little sailboats that looked like white paper napkins. On the beach, women in bikinis lounged around in sun glasses, or else played badminton. I looked at all the posters in the window, including those for Germany and Merrie England, but I kept going back to that grinning sun, the beach, the women, and the little boats. Finally I combed my hair in the reflection from the window, straightened my shoulders, and went on to the florist's.

The next morning Frank Klovee came to work wearing slacks, white shirt and tie. He said if any of us wanted to go see Harry off it was all right with him. Most of the guys went home to change, took in the funeral, and then took the rest of the afternoon off. Jimmy had set up a little buffet at the Red Fox in honor of Harry. He had different kinds of dip, potato chips and sandwiches. I didn't go to the funeral but I did drop by the Red Fox later in the afternoon. Little Judith was there, sure. She was dressed up and moving around the place like she'd had a heavy dose of shell shock. Mike Demarest was there too, and I could see him looking her over from time to time. She went from one guy to another talking about Harry and saying things like, "Harry thought the world of you, Gus." Or, "Harry would have wanted it that way." Or, "Harry would have liked that part best. Harry was just that sort." Two or three guys hugged her and patted her on the hips and carried on so that I almost asked them to leave off. A few old pods drifted in, guys that Harry probably hadn't exchanged a dozen words with in his life—if he'd ever even laid eyes on them—and said what a tragedy it was, and threw down beer and sandwiches. Little Judith and I stayed around till the place emptied out around seven. Then I took her home.

You've probably guessed some of the rest of the story by now. Little Judith and I started keeping company after Harry's death. We went to the movies nearly every night and then to a bar or else to her place. We only went back to the Red Fox once, and then we decided not to go there any more, but to go to new places instead —places where she and Harry had never been. One Sunday not long after the funeral the two of us went out to Golden Gate Cemetery to put a pot of flowers on Harry's grave. But they hadn't put his marker in yet, so we spent an hour looking for it and were still not able to find the goddamn grave. Little Judith kept running around from one spot to another calling, "Here it is! Here it is!" But the plot always turned out to belong to somebody else. We finally left, both of us feeling depressed.

In August we drove down to L.A. to have a look at the boat. It was a fine piece of work Harry's uncle had kept it in prime shape and Tomás, the Mexican boy who looked after it, said he wouldn't be afraid to take it around the world. Little Judith and I just looked at it and then looked at each other. It's seldom anything turns out to be better than you expected it to be. Usually it's the other way around. But that's the way it was with this boat—better than anything we'd dreamed. On our way back to San Francisco we decided to take it on a little cruise the next month. And so we set out on our trip in September, just before the Labor Day weekend.

As I said, a lot of things have changed since Harry's death. Even Little Judith is out of the picture now, gone in a way that is tragic and still has me wondering. It was somewhere off the Baja coast that it happened: Little Judith, who couldn't swim a stroke, came up missing. We figured she fell overboard during the night. What she was doing up on deck so late, or what caused her to fall overboard, neither Tomás nor I know. All we know is that the next morning she was gone and neither of us saw anything or heard her cry out. She simply disappeared. That is the truth, so help me, and what I told the police when we put in at Guaymas a few days later. My wife, I told them—for luckily we'd married just before leaving San Francisco. It was to have been our honeymoon trip.

I said things have changed since Harry's death. Now here I am in Mazatlan and Tomás is showing me some of the sights. Things you never thought existed back in the States. Our next stop is Manzanillo, Tomás's home town. Then Acapulco. We intend to keep going until the money runs out, then put in and work for a while, then set out again. It occurs to me that I'm doing things the way Harry would have wanted. But who can tell about that now?

Sometimes I think I was born to be a rover.

THE PHEASANT

Gerald Weber didn't have any words left in him. He kept quiet and drove the car. Shirley Lennart had stayed awake at first, for the novelty of it more than anything, the fact of being alone with him for any length of time. She'd put several cassettes on to play—Crystal Gayle, Chuck Mangione, Willie Nelson—and then later, toward morning, had begun dialing the radio from one station to another, picking up world and local news, brief weather and farm reports, even an early morning question-and-answer program on the effects of marijuana smoking on nursing mothers, anything to fill in the long silences. From time to time, smoking, she looked across at him through the dark gloom of the big car. Somewhere between San Luis Obispo and Potter, California, a hundred and fifty miles or so from her summer house at Carmel, she gave up Gerald Weber as a bad investment — she'd made others, she reflected wearily—and fell asleep on the seat.

He could hear her ragged breathing over the sound of the air that rushed by outside. He turned off the radio and was glad for the privacy. It had been a mistake to leave Hollywood in the middle of the night for a three-hundred-mile drive, but that night, two days before his thirtieth birthday, he'd felt at loose ends and suggested that they drive up to her beach house for a few days. It was ten o'clock and they were still drinking martinis, though they'd moved out to the patio that overlooked the city. "Why not?" she'd said, stirring the drink with her finger and looking at him where he stood against the balcony railing. "Let's. I think it's the best idea you've had all week," licking the gin off her finger.

He took his eyes off the road. She didn't look asleep, she looked unconscious, or seriously injured—as if she'd fallen out of a building. She lay twisted in the seat, one leg doubled under and the other hanging over the seat almost to the floor. The skirt was pulled above her thighs, exposing the tops of the nylons, the garter

147

belt, and the flesh in between. Her head lay on the arm rest and her mouth was open.

It had rained off and on through the night. Now, just as it began to turn light, the rain stopped, although the highway was still damp and black and he could see small puddles of water lying in the depressions in the open fields on either side of the road. He wasn't tired yet. He felt all right, considering. He was glad to be doing something. It felt good to sit there behind the wheel, driving, not having to think.

He had just turned off the headlights and decreased his speed a little when he saw the pheasant out of the corner of his eye. It was flying low and fast and at an angle that might take it into the path of the car. He touched the brake, then increased his speed and tightened his grip on the wheel. The bird struck the left headlamp with a loud *thunk*. It spun up past the windshield, trailing feathers and a stream of shit.

"Oh my God," he said, appalled at what he'd done.

"What's happened?" she said, sitting up heavily, wide-eyed and startled.

"I hit something...a pheasant." He could hear the glass from the broken headlamp tinkling on the pavement as he braked the car.

He pulled onto the shoulder and got out. The air was damp and cold and he buttoned his sweater as he bent over to inspect the damage. Except for a few jagged pieces of glass which he tried for a minute with trembling fingers to loosen and work out, the head-lamp was gone. There was also a small dent in the left front fender. In the dent, a smear of blood coated the metal and several dun-colored feathers were pressed into the blood. It was a hen pheasant, he'd seen that the moment before the impact.

Shirley leaned over to his side of the car and pressed the button for the window. She was still half-asleep. "Gerry?" she called to him.

"Just a minute. Just stay in the car," he said.

"I wasn't about to get out," she said. "Just hurry, I mean."

He walked back along the shoulder. A truck went by throwing up a mist of spray, and the driver looked out of the cab at him as he roared past. Gerry hunched his shoulders against the cold and kept walking until he came to the sprinkling of broken glass in the road. He walked further, looking closely into the wet grass beside the road, until he found the bird. He couldn't bring himself to touch it, but he looked at it for a minute; crumpled, its eyes open, a bright spot of blood on its beak.

When he was back in the car, Shirley said, "I didn't know what had happened. Did it do much damage?"

"It knocked out a headlight and made a little dent in the fender," he said. He looked back the way they'd come, and then pulled out onto the road.

"Did it kill it?" she said. "I mean, it must have, of course. I suppose it didn't have a chance."

He looked at her and then back at the road. "We were going seventy miles an hour."

"How long have I been asleep?"

When he didn't answer, she said, "I have a headache. I have a bad headache. How far are we from Carmel?"

"A couple of hours," he said.

"I'd like something to eat and some coffee. Maybe that'll make my head feel better," she said.

"We'll stop in the next town," he said.

She turned the rearview mirror and studied her face. She touched here and there under her eyes with her finger. Then she yawned and turned on the radio. She began to spin the knob.

He thought about the pheasant. It had happened very fast, but it was clear to him he'd hit the bird deliberately. "How well do you really know me?" he said.

"What do you mean?" she said. She let the radio alone for a minute and leaned back against the seat.

"I just said, How well do you know me?"

"I don't have any idea what you mean."

He said, "Just how well do you know me? That's all I'm asking."

"Why do you ask me that at this time of the morning?"

"We're just talking. I just asked you how well you knew me. Would I"—how should he put it?—"am I trustworthy, for instance? Do you trust me?" It wasn't clear to him what he was asking, but he felt on the edge of something.

"Is it important?" she said. She looked at him steadily.

He shrugged. "If you don't think it is, then I guess it isn't." He gave his attention back to the road. At least in the beginning, he thought, there'd been some affection. They began living together because she had suggested it for one thing, and because at the time he'd met her, at the party of a friend in a Pacific Palisades apartment, he'd wanted the kind of life he imagined she could give him. She had money and she had connections. Connections were more important than money. But money and connections both—that was unbeatable. As for him, he was just out of graduate studies at UCLA, a drama major—wasn't the city filled with them though—and, except for university theater productions, an actor without a salaried role to his credit. He was also broke. She was older by twelve years, had been married and divorced twice, but she had some money and she took him to parties where he met people. As a result, he'd landed a few minor roles. He could call himself an actor at long last, even if he didn't have more than a month or two month's work each year. The rest of the time, these last three years, he'd spent lying in the sun near her pool, or at parties, or else running here and there with Shirley.

"Let me ask you this then," he went on. "Do you think I'd act, that I'd ever do something against my own best interests?"

She looked at him and tapped a tooth with her thumbnail.

"Well?" he said. It still wasn't clear to him where this might lead. But he intended to keep on with it.

"Well, what?" she said.

"You heard me."

"I think you would, Gerald. I think you would if you thought it was important enough at the time. Now don't ask me any more questions, okay?"

The sun was out now. The clouds had broken up. He began to see signs announcing various services in the next town. There was more traffic on the road. The wet fields on either side looked freshly green and sparkled in the early morning sun.

She smoked her cigarette and stared out the window. She wondered if she should spend the energy to change the subject. But she was becoming irritated too. She was sick of this whole thing. It was too bad she'd agreed to come with him. She should've stayed in Hollywood. She didn't like people who were forever trying to find themselves, the brooding, introspective bit.

Then she said, "Look! Look at those places," she exclaimed.

Out in the fields on their left were sections of portable barracks, housing for the farmworkers. The barracks stood on blocks two or three feet off the ground, waiting to be trucked to another location. There were twenty-five or thirty such barracks. They had been raised off the ground and left standing so that some of the barracks faced the road and some of them were facing in other directions. It looked as if an upheaval had taken place.

"Look at that," she said as they sped past.

"John Steinbeck," he said. "Something out of Steinbeck."

"What?" she said. "Oh, Steinbeck. Yes, that's right. Steinbeck."

He blinked his eyes and imagined he saw the pheasant. He remembered his foot punching down on the accelerator as he tried to hit the bird. He opened his mouth to say something. But he couldn't find any words. He was amazed, and at the same time deeply moved and ashamed, at the sudden impulse—which he'd acted upon—to kill the pheasant. His fingers stiffened on the wheel.

"What would you say if I told you I killed that pheasant intentionally? That I tried to hit it?"

She gazed at him for a minute without any interest. She didn't say anything. Something became clear to him then. Partly, he supposed later, it was a result of the look of bored indifference she turned on him, and partly it was a consequence of his own state of mind. But he suddenly understood that he no longer had any values. No frame of reference, was the phrase that ran through his mind.

"Is it true?" she said.

He nodded. "It could have been dangerous. It could have gone through the windshield. But it's more than that," he said.

"I'm sure it's more than that. If you say so, Gerry. But it doesn't surprise me, if that's what you think. I'm not surprised," she said. "Nothing about you surprises me any more. You get your kicks, don't you?"

They were entering Potter. He cut his speed and began looking for the restaurant he'd seen advertised on the billboard. He located it a few blocks into the downtown area and pulled up in front onto the gravelled parking area. It was still early in the morning. Inside the restaurant, heads turned in their direction as he eased the big car to a stop and set the brake. He took the key from the ignition. They turned in the seat and looked at each other.

"I'm not hungry any more," she said. "You know something? You take away my appetite."

"I take away my own appetite," he said.

She continued to stare at him. "Do you know what you'd better do, Gerald? You'd better do something."

"I'll think of something." He opened the car door and got out. He bent down in front of the car and examined the smashed headlamp and the dented fender. Then he went around to her side of the car and opened the door for her. She hesitated, then got out of the car.

"Keys," she said. "The car keys, please."

He felt as if they were doing a scene and this was the fifth or sixth take. But it still wasn't clear what was going to happen next. He was suddenly tired through to his bones, but he felt high too and on the edge of something. He gave her the keys. She closed her hand and made a fist.

He said, "I suppose I'll say goodbye then, Shirley. If that isn't too melodramatic." They stood there in front of the restaurant. "I'm going to try and get my life in order," he said. "For one thing, find a job, a real job. Just not see anybody for a while. Okay? No tears, okay? We'll stay friends, if you want. We had some good times, right?"

"Gerald, you are nothing to me," Shirley said. "You're an ass. You can go to hell, you son of a bitch."

Inside the restaurant, two waitresses and a few men in coveralls all moved to the front window to watch after the woman outside slapped the man on his cheek with the back of her hand. The people inside were at first shocked and then amused with the scene. Now the woman in the parking area was pointing down the road and shaking her finger. Very dramatic. But the man had already started walking. He didn't look back, either. The people inside couldn't hear what the woman was saying, but they thought they had the picture since the man kept walking.

"God, she let him have it, didn't she?" one of the waitresses spoke up. "He got the boot and no mistake."

"He don't know how to treat them," said a trucker who had watched everything. "He should turn around and just knock hell out of her."

WHERE IS EVERYONE?

I've seen some things. I was going over to my mother's to stay a few nights, but just as I came to the top of the stairs I looked and she was on the sofa kissing a man. It was summer, the door was open, and the color TV was playing.

My mother is sixty-five and lonely. She belongs to a singles club. But even so, knowing all this, it was hard. I stood at the top of the stairs with my hand on the railing and watched as the man pulled her deeper into the kiss. It was Sunday, about five in the afternoon. People from the apartment house were in the pool. I went back down the stairs and out to my car.

A lot has happened since that afternoon, and on the whole things are better now. But during those days, when my mother was putting out to men she'd just met, I was out of work, drinking, and crazy. My kids were crazy, and my wife was crazy and having a "thing" with an unemployed aerospace engineer she'd met at AA. He was crazy too. His name was Ross and he had five or six kids. He walked with a limp from a gunshot wound his first wife had given him. He didn't have a wife now; he wanted my wife. I don't know what we were all thinking of in those days. The second wife had come and gone, but it was his first wife who had shot him in the thigh some years back, giving him the limp, and who now had him in and out of court, or in jail, every six months or so for not meeting his support payments. I wish him well now. But it was different then. More than once in those days I mentioned weapons. I'd say to my wife, I'd shout it, "I'm going to kill him!" But nothing ever happened. Things lurched on. I never met the man, though we talked on the phone a few times. I did find a couple of pictures of him once when I was going through my wife's purse. He was a little guy, not too little, and he had a moustache and was wearing a striped jersey, waiting for a kid to come down the slide. In the other picture he was standing against a house—my house?

155

I couldn't tell—with his arms crossed, dressed up, wearing a tie. Ross, you son of a bitch, I hope you're okay now. I hope things are better for you too.

The last time he'd been jailed, a month before that Sunday, I found out from my daughter that her mother had gone bail for him. Daughter Kate, who was fifteen, didn't take to this any better than I did. It wasn't that she had any loyalty to me in this—she had no loyalties to me or her mother in anything and was only too willing to sell either one of us down the river. No, it was that there was a serious cash-flow problem in the house and if money went to Ross, there'd be that much less for what she needed. So Ross was on her list now. Also, she didn't like his kids, she'd said, but she'd told me once before that in general Ross was all right, even funny and interesting when he wasn't drinking. He'd even told her fortune.

He spent his time repairing things, now that he could no longer hold a job in the aerospace industry. But I'd seen his house from the outside; and the place looked like a dumping ground, with all kinds and makes of old appliances and equipment that would never wash or cook or play again—all of it just standing in his open garage and on his drive and in the front yard. He also kept some broken-down cars around that he liked to tinker on. In the first stages of their affair my wife had told me he "collected antique cars." Those were her words. I'd seen some of his cars parked in front of his house when I'd driven by there trying to see what I could see. Old 1950s and 1960s, dented cars with torn seat covers. They were junkers, that's all. I knew. I had his number. We had things in common, more than just driving old cars and trying to hold on for dear life to the same woman. Still, handyman or not, he couldn't manage to tune my wife's car properly or fix our TV set when it broke down and we lost the picture. We had volume, but no picture. If we wanted to get the news, we'd have to sit around the screen at night and listen to the set. I'd drink and make some crack to my kids about Mr. Fixit. Even now I don't know if my wife believed that stuff or not, about antique cars and such. But she cared for him. I guess she loved him even; that's pretty clear now.

They'd met when Cynthia was trying to stay sober and was going to meetings three or four times a week. I had been in and out of AA for several months, though when Cynthia met Ross I was out and drinking a fifth a day of anything I could get my hands on. But as I heard Cynthia say to someone over the phone about me, I'd had the exposure to AA and knew where to go when I really wanted help. Ross had been in AA and then had gone back to drinking again. I think Cynthia felt that maybe there was more hope for him than for me and so went to the meetings to keep herself sober, then went over to cook for him or clean his house. His kids weren't of help to him in this regard. Nobody lifted a hand around his house except Cynthia when she was there. But the less his kids pitched in, the more he loved them. It was strange. It was the opposite with me. I hated my kids during this time. I'd be on the sofa with a glass of vodka and grapefruit juice when one of them would come in from school and slam the door. One afternoon I screamed and got into a scuffle with my son. Cynthia had to break it up when I threatened to knock him to pieces. I said I would kill him. I said, "I'll kill you and not bat an eye."

Madness.

The kids, Katy and Mike, were only too happy to take advantage of this crumbling situation. They seemed to thrive on the threats and bullying they inflicted on each other and on us—the violence and dismay, the general bedlam. Right now, thinking about it even from this distance, it makes me set my heart against them. I remember years before, before I turned to drinking full time, reading an extraordinary scene in a novel by an Italian named Italo Svevo. The narrator's father was dying and the family had gathered around the bed, weeping and waiting for the old man to expire, when he opened his eyes to look at each of them for a last time. When his gaze fell on the narrator he suddenly stirred and something came into his eyes; and with his last burst of strength he raised up, flung himself across the bed, and slapped the face of his son as hard as he could. Then he fell back onto the bed and died. I often imagined my own deathbed scene in those days, and I saw myself doing the same thing—only I would hope to have the strength to slap each of my kids and my last words for them would be what only a dying man would have the courage to utter.

But they saw craziness on every side, and it suited their purpose, I was convinced. They fattened on it. They liked being able to call the shots, having the upper hand while we bungled along letting them work on our guilt. They might have been inconvenienced from time to time, but they ran things their way. They weren't embarrassed or put out by any of the activities that went on in our house either. To the contrary. It gave them something to talk about with their friends. I've heard them regaling their pals with the most frightful stories, howling with laughter as they spilled out the lurid details of what was happening to me and their mother. Except for being financially dependent on Cynthia, who still somehow had a teaching job and a monthly paycheck, they flat-out ran the show. And that's what it was—a show.

Once Mike locked his mother out of the house after she'd stayed overnight at Ross's house....I don't know where I was that night, probably at my mother's. I'd sleep over there sometimes. I'd eat supper with her and she'd tell me how she worried about all of us; then we'd watch TV and try to talk about something else, try to hold a normal conversation about something other than my family situation. She'd make a bed for me on her sofa—the same sofa she used to make love on, I supposed, but I'd sleep there anyway and be grateful. Cynthia came home at seven o'clock one morning to get dressed for school and found that Mike had locked all the doors and windows and wouldn't let her in the house. She stood outside his window and begged him to let her in—please, please, so she could dress and go to school, for if she lost her job what then? Where would he be? Where would any of us be then? He said, "You don't live here any more. Why should I let you in?" That's what he said to her, standing behind his window, his face all stopped up with rage. (She told me this later when she was drunk and I was sober and holding her hands and letting her talk.) "You don't live here," he said.

"Please, please, please, Mike," she pleaded. "Let me in."

He let her in and she swore at him. Like that, he punched her hard on the shoulders several times—whop, whop, whop—then hit her on top of the head and generally worked her over. Finally she was able to change clothes, fix her face, and rush off to school.

All this happened not too long ago, three years about. It was something in those days.

I left my mother with the man on her sofa and drove around for a while, not wanting to go home and not wanting to sit in a bar that day either.

Sometimes Cynthia and I would talk about things—"reviewing the situation," we'd call it. But now and then on rare occasions we'd talk a little about things that bore no relation to the situation. One afternoon we were in the living room and she said, "When I was pregnant with Mike you carried me to the bathroom when I was so sick and pregnant I couldn't get out of bed. You carried me. No one else will ever do that, no one else could ever love me in that way, that much. We have that, no matter what. We've loved each other like nobody else could or ever will love the other again."

We looked at each other. Maybe we touched hands, I don't recall. Then I remembered the half-pint of whisky or vodka or gin or Scotch or tequila that I'd hidden under the very sofa cushion we were sitting on and I began to hope she might soon have to get up and move around—go to the kitchen, the bathroom, out to clean the garage.

"Maybe you could make us some coffee," I said. "A pot of coffee might be nice."

"Would you eat something? I can fix some soup."

"Maybe I could eat something, but I'll for sure drink a cup of coffee."

She went out to the kitchen. I waited until I heard her begin to run water. Then I reached under the cushion for the bottle, unscrewed the lid, and drank.

I never told these things at AA. I never said much at the meetings. I'd "pass" as they called it when it came your turn to speak and you didn't say anything except "I'll pass tonight, thanks." But I would listen and shake my head and laugh in recognition of the awful stories I heard. Usually I was drunk when I went to those meetings. You're scared and you need something more than cookies and instant coffee.

But those conversations touching on love or the past were rare. If we talked, we talked about business, survival, the bottom line of things. Money. Where is the money going to come from? The telephone was on the way out, the lights and gas threatened. What about Katy? She needs clothes. Her grades. That boyfriend of hers is a biker. Mike. What's going to happen to Mike? What's going to happen to us all? "My God," she'd say. But God wasn't having any of it. He'd washed his hands of us.

I wanted Mike to join the army, navy, or the coast guard. He was impossible. A dangerous character. Even Ross felt the army would be good for him, Cynthia had told me, and she hadn't liked him telling her that a bit. But I was pleased to hear this and to find out that Ross and I were in agreement on the matter. Ross went up a peg in my estimation. But it angered Cynthia because, miserable as Mike was to have around, despite his violent side, she thought it was just a phase that would soon pass. She didn't want him in the army. But Ross told Cynthia that Mike belonged in the army where he'd learn respect and manners. He told her this after there'd been a pushing and shoving match out in his drive in the early morning hours when Mike had thrown him down on the pavement.

Ross loved Cynthia, but he also had a twenty-two-year-old girl named Beverly who was pregnant with his baby, though Ross assured Cynthia he loved her, not Beverly. They didn't even sleep together any longer, he told Cynthia, but Beverly was carrying his baby and he loved all his children, even the unborn, and he couldn't just give her the boot, could he? He wept when he told all this to Cynthia. He was drunk. (Someone was always drunk in those days.) I can imagine the scene.

Ross had graduated from California Polytechnic Institute and gone right to work at the NASA operation in Mountain View. He worked there for ten years, until it all fell in on him. I never met him, as I said, but we talked on the phone several times, about one thing and another. I called him once when I was drunk and Cynthia and I were debating some sad point or another. One of his children answered the phone and when Ross came on the line I asked him whether, if I pulled out (I had no intention of pulling out, of course; it was just harassment), he intended to support Cynthia and our kids. He said he was carving a roast, that's what he said, and they were just going to sit down and eat their dinner, he and his children. Could he call me back? I hung up. When he called, after an hour or so, I'd forgotten about the earlier call.

Cynthia answered the phone and said, "Yes," and then "Yes" again, and I knew it was Ross and that he was asking if I was drunk. I grabbed the phone. "Well, are you going to support them or not?" He said he was sorry for his part in all of this but, no, he guessed he couldn't support them. "So it's No, you can't support them," I said, and looked at Cynthia as if this should settle everything. He said, "Yes, it's no." But Cynthia didn't bat an eye. I figured later they'd already talked that situation over thoroughly, so it was no surprise. She already knew.

He was in his mid-thirties when he went under. I used to make fun of him when I had the chance. I called him "the weasel," after his photograph. "That's what your mother's boyfriend looks like," I'd say to my kids if they were around and we were talking. "Like a weasel." We'd laugh. Or else "Mr. Fixit." That was my favorite name for him. God bless and keep you, Ross. I don't hold anything against you now. But in those days when I called him the weasel or Mr. Fixit and threatened his life, he was something of a fallen hero to my kids and to Cynthia too, I suppose, because he'd helped put men on the moon. He'd worked, I was told time and again, on the moon project shots, and he was close friends with Buzz Aldren and Neil Armstrong. He'd told Cynthia, and Cynthia had told the kids, who'd told me, that when the astronauts came to town he was going to introduce them. But they never came to town, or if they did they forgot to contact Ross. Soon after the moon probes, fortune's wheel turned and Ross's drinking increased. He began missing work. Sometime then the troubles with his first wife started. Toward the end he began taking the drink to work with him in a thermos. It's a modern operation out there, I've seen it—cafeteria lines, executive dining rooms, and the like, Mr. Coffee's in every office. But he brought his own thermos to work, and after a while people began to know and to talk. He was laid off, or else he quit—nobody could ever give me a straight answer when I asked. He kept drinking, of course. You do that. Then he commenced working on ruined appliances and doing TV repair work and fixing cars. He was interested in astrology, auras, I Ching—that business. I don't doubt that he was bright enough and interesting and quirky, like most of our ex-friends. I told Cynthia I was sure she wouldn't care for him (I couldn't bring myself to use the word "love" about that relationship) if he wasn't, basically, a good man. "One of us," was how I put it, trying to be large about it. He wasn't a bad or an evil man, Ross. "No one's evil," I said once to Cynthia when we were discussing my own affair.

My dad died in his sleep, drunk, eight years ago. It was a Friday night and he was fifty-four years old. He came home from work at the sawmill, took some sausage out of the freezer for his breakfast the next morning, and sat down at the kitchen table, where he opened a quart of Four Roses. He was in good enough spirits in those days, glad to be back on a job after being out of work for three or four years with blood poisoning and then something that caused him to have shock treatments. (I was married and living in another town during that time. I had the kids and a job, enough troubles of my own, so I couldn't follow his too closely.) That night he moved into the living room with his bottle, a bowl of ice cubes and a glass, and drank and watched TV until my mother came in from work at the coffee shop.

They had a few words about the whisky. She didn't drink much herself. When I was grown, I only saw her drink at Thanksgiving, Christmas, and New Year's Eve—eggnog or buttered rums, and then never too many. The one time she had had too much to drink, years before (I heard this from my dad who laughed about it when he told it), they'd gone to a little place outside Eureka and she'd had a great many whisky sours. Just as they got into the car to leave, she started to get sick and had to open the door. Somehow her false teeth came out, the car moved forward a little, and a tire passed over her dentures. After that she never drank except on holidays and then never to excess.

My dad kept on drinking that Friday night and tried to ignore my mother, who sat out in the kitchen and smoked and tried to write a letter to her sister in Little Rock. Finally he got up and went to bed. My mother went to bed not long after, when she was sure he was asleep. She said later she noticed nothing out of the ordinary except maybe his snoring seemed heavier and deeper and she couldn't get him to turn on his side. But she went to sleep. She woke up when my dad's sphincter muscles and bladder let go. It was just sunrise. Birds were singing. My dad was still on his back, eyes closed and mouth open. My mother looked at him and cried his name.

I kept driving around. It was dark by now. I drove by my house, every light ablaze, but Cynthia's car wasn't in the drive. I went to a bar where I sometimes drank and called home. Katy answered and said her mother wasn't there, and where was I? She needed five dollars. I shouted something and hung up. Then I called collect to a woman eight hundred miles away whom I hadn't seen in months, a good woman who, the last time I'd seen her, had said she would pray for me.

She accepted the charges. She asked where I was. She asked how I was. "Are you all right?" she said.

We talked. I asked about her husband. He'd been a friend of mine and was now living away from her and the children.

"He's still in Portland," she said. "How did all this happen to us?" she asked. "We started out good people." We talked a while longer; then she said she still loved me and that she would continue to pray for me.

"Pray for me," I said. "Yes." Then we said good-bye and hung up.

Later I called home again, but this time no one answered. I dialed my mother's number. She picked up the phone on the first ring, her voice cautious, as if expecting trouble.

"It's me," I said. "I'm sorry to be calling."

"No, no, honey, I was up," she said. "Where are you? Is anything the matter? I thought you were coming over today. I looked for you. Are you at home?"

"I'm not at home," I said. "I just called there."

"Old Ken was over here today," she went on, "that old bastard. He came over this afternoon. I haven't seen him in a month and he just shows up, the old thing. I don't like him. All he wants to do is talk about himself and brag on himself and how he lived on Guam and had three girlfriends at the same time and how he's traveled to this place and that place. He's just an old braggart, that's all he is. I met him at that dance I told you about, but I don't like him."

"Is it all right if I come over?" I said.

"Honey, why don't you? I'll fix us something to eat. I'm hungry myself. I haven't eaten anything since this afternoon. Old Ken brought some Colonel Sanders over this afternoon. Come over and I'll fix us some scrambled eggs. Do you want me to come get you? Honey, are you all right?"

I drove over. She kissed me when I came in the door. I turned my face. I hated for her to smell the vodka. The TV was on.

"Wash your hands," she said as she studied me. "It's ready."

Later she made a bed for me on the sofa. I went into the bathroom. She kept a pair of my dad's pajamas in there. I took them out of the drawer, looked at them, and began undressing. When I came out she was in the kitchen. I fixed the pillow and lay down. She finished with what she was doing, turned off the kitchen light, and sat down at the end of the sofa.

"Honey, I don't want to be the one to tell you this," she said. "It hurts me to tell you, but even the kids know it and they've told me. We've talked about it. But Cynthia is seeing another man."

"That's okay," I said. "I know that," I said and looked at the TV. "His name is Ross and he's an alcoholic. He's like me."

"Honey, you're going to have to do something for yourself," she said.

"I know it," I said. I kept looking at the TV.

She leaned over and hugged me. She held me a minute. Then she let go and wiped her eyes. "I'll get you up in the morning," she said.

"I don't have much to do tomorrow. I might sleep in a while after you go." I thought: after you get up, after you've gone to the bathroom and gotten dressed, then I'll get into your bed and lie there and doze and listen to your radio out in the kitchen giving the news and weather.

"Honey, I'm so worried about you."

"Don't worry," I said. I shook my head.

"You get some rest now," she said. "You need to sleep."

"I'll sleep. I'm very sleepy."

"Watch TV as long as you want," she said.

I nodded.

She bent and kissed me. Her lips seemed bruised and swollen. She drew the blanket over me. Then she went into her bedroom. She left the door open, and in a minute I could hear her snoring.

I lay there staring at the TV. There were images of uniformed men on the screen, a low murmur, then tanks and a man using a flamethrower. I couldn't hear the sound, but I didn't want to get up. I kept staring until I felt my eyes close. But I woke up with a start, the pajamas damp with sweat. A snowy light filled the room. There was a roaring coming at me. The room clamored. I lay there. I didn't move.

SO MUCH WATER
SO CLOSE TO HOME

My husband eats with good appetite but he seems tired, edgy. He chews slowly, arms on the table, and stares at something across the room. He looks at me and looks away again. He wipes his mouth on the napkin. He shrugs and goes on eating. Something has come between us though he would like me to believe otherwise.

"What are you staring at me for?" he asks. "What is it?" he says and puts his fork down.

"Was I staring?" I say and shake my head stupidly, stupidly.

The telephone rings. "Don't answer it," he says.

"It might be your mother," I say. "Dean—it might be something about Dean."

"Watch and see," he says.

I pick up the receiver and listen for a minute. He stops eating. I bite my lip and hang up.

"What did I tell you?" he says. He starts to eat again, then throws the napkin onto his plate. "Goddamn it, why can't people mind their own business? Tell me what I did wrong and I'll listen! It's not fair. She was dead, wasn't she? There were other men there besides me. We talked it over and we all decided. We'd only just got there. We'd walked for hours. We couldn't just turn around, we were five miles from the car. It was opening day. What the hell, I don't see anything wrong. No, I don't. And don't look at me that way, do you hear? I won't have you passing judgment on me. Not you."

"You know," I say and shake my head.

"What do I know, Claire? Tell me. Tell me what I know. I don't know anything except one thing: you hadn't better get worked up over this." He gives me what he thinks is a *meaningful* look. "She was dead, dead, dead, do you hear?" he says after a minute. "It's a damn shame, I agree. She was a young girl and it's a shame, and I'm

167

sorry, as sorry as anyone else, but she was dead, Claire, dead. Now let's leave it alone. Please, Claire. Let's leave it alone now."

"That's the point," I say. "She was dead. But don't you see? She needed help."

"I give up," he says and raises his hands. He pushes his chair away from the table, takes his cigarettes and goes out to the patio with a can of beer. He walks back and forth for a minute and then sits in a lawn chair and picks up the paper once more. His name is there on the first page along with the names of his friends, the other men who made the "grisly find."

I close my eyes for a minute and hold onto the drainboard. I must not dwell on this any longer. I must get over it, put it out of sight, out of mind, etc., and "go on." I open my eyes. Despite everything, knowing all that may be in store, I rake my arm across the drainboard and send the dishes and glasses smashing and scattering across the floor.

He doesn't move. I know he has heard, he raises his head as if listening, but he doesn't move otherwise, doesn't turn around to look. I hate him for that, for not moving. He waits a minute, then draws on his cigarette and leans back in the chair. I pity him for listening, detached, and then settling back and drawing on his cigarette. The wind takes the smoke out of his mouth in a thin stream. Why do I notice that? He can never know how much I pity him for that, for sitting still and listening, and letting the smoke stream out of his mouth. . . .

He planned his fishing trip into the mountains last Sunday, a week before the Memorial Day weekend. He and Gordon Johnson, Mel Dorn, Vern Williams. They play poker, bowl, and fish together. They fish together every spring and early summer, the first two or three months of the season, before family vacations, little league baseball, and visiting relatives can intrude. They are decent men, family men, responsible at their jobs. They have sons and daughters who go to school with our son, Dean. On Friday afternoon these four men left for a three day fishing trip to the Naches River. They parked the car in the mountains and hiked several miles to where they wanted to fish. They carried their bedrolls, food and cooking utensils, their playing cards, their whisky. The first evening at the river, even before they could set up camp, Mel Dorn found the girl floating face down in the river, nude, lodged near the shore in some branches. He called the other men and they all came to look at her. They talked about what to do. One of the men—Stuart didn't say which—perhaps it was Vern Williams, he is a heavy-set, easy man who laughs often—one of them thought they should start back to the car at once. The others stirred the sand with their shoes and said they felt inclined to stay. They pleaded fatigue, the late hour, the fact that the girl "wasn't going anywhere." In the end they all decided to stay. They went ahead and set up the camp and built a fire and drank their whisky. They drank a lot of whisky and when the moon came up they talked about the girl. Someone thought they should do something to prevent the body from floating away. Somehow they thought that this might create a problem for them if it floated away during the night. They took flashlights and stumbled down to the river. The wind was up, a cold wind, and waves from the river lapped the sandy bank. One of the men, I don't know who, it might have been Stuart, he could have done it, waded into the water and took the girl by the fingers and pulled her, still face down, closer to shore, into shallow water, and then took a piece of nylon cord and tied it around her wrist and then secured the cord to tree roots, all the while the flashlights of the other men played over the girl's body. Afterwards, they went back to camp and drank more whisky. Then they went to sleep. The next morning, Saturday, they cooked breakfast, drank lots of coffee, more whisky, and then split up to fish, two men upriver, two men down.

That night, after they had cooked their fish and potatoes and had more coffee and whisky, they took their dishes down to the river and rinsed them off a few yards from where the body lay in the water. They drank again and then they took out their cards and played and drank until they couldn't see the cards any longer. Vern Williams went to sleep, but the others told coarse stories and spoke of vulgar or dishonest escapades out of their past, and no one mentioned the girl until Gordon Johnson, who'd forgotten for a minute, commented on the firmness of the trout they'd caught, and the terrible coldness of the river water. They stopped talking then but continued to drink until one of them tripped and fell cursing against the lantern, and then they climbed into their sleeping bags.

The next morning they got up late, drank more whisky, fished a little as they kept drinking whisky. Then, at one o'clock in the afternoon, Sunday, a day earlier than they'd planned, they decided to leave. They took down their tents, rolled their sleeping bags, gathered their pans, pots, fish and fishing gear, and hiked out. They didn't look at the girl again before they left. When they reached the car they drove the highway in silence until they came to a telephone. Stuart made the call to the sheriff's office while the others stood around in the hot sun and listened. He gave the man on the other end of the line all of their names—they had nothing to hide, they weren't ashamed of anything—and agreed to wait at the service station until someone could come for more detailed directions and individual statements.

He came home at eleven o'clock that night. I was asleep but woke when I heard him in the kitchen. I found him leaning against the refrigerator drinking a can of beer. He put his heavy arms around me and rubbed his hands up and down my back, the same hands he'd left with two days before, I thought.

In bed he put his hands on me again and then waited, as if thinking of something else. I turned slightly and then moved my legs. Afterwards, I know he stayed awake for a long time, for he was awake when I fell asleep; and later, when I stirred for a minute, opening my eyes at a slight noise, a rustle of sheets, it was almost daylight outside, birds were singing, and he was on his back smoking and looking at the curtained window. Half-asleep I said his name, but he didn't answer. I fell asleep again.

He was up this morning before I could get out of bed—to see if there was anything about it in the paper, I suppose. The telephone began to ring shortly after eight o'clock.

"Go to hell," I heard him shout into the receiver. The telephone rang again a minute later, and I hurried into the kitchen. "I have nothing else to add to what I've already said to the sheriff. That's right!" He slammed down the receiver.

"What is going on?" I said, alarmed.

"Sit down," he said slowly. His fingers scraped, scraped against his stubble of whiskers. "I have to tell you something. Something happened while we were fishing." We sat across from each other at the table, and then he told me.

I drank coffee and stared at him as he spoke. Then I read the account in the newspaper that he shoved across the table: "... unidentified girl eighteen to twenty-four years of age...body three to five days in the water...rape a possible motive...preliminary results show death by strangulation...cuts and bruises on her breasts and pelvic area...autopsy...rape, pending further investigation."

"You've got to understand," he said. "Don't look at me like that. Be careful now, I mean it. Take it easy, Claire."

"Why didn't you tell me last night?" I asked.

"I just...didn't. What do you mean?" he said.

"You know what I mean," I said. I looked at his hands, the broad fingers, knuckles covered with hair, moving, lighting a cigarette now, fingers that had moved over me, into me last night.

He shrugged. "What difference does it make, last night, this morning? It was late. You were sleepy, I thought I'd wait until this morning to tell you." He looked out to the patio: a robin flew from the lawn to the picnic table and preened its feathers.

"It isn't true," I said. "You didn't leave her there like that?"

He turned quickly and said, "What'd I do? Listen to me carefully now, once and for all. Nothing happened. I have nothing to be sorry for or feel guilty about. Do you hear me?"

I got up from the table and went to Dean's room. He was awake and in his pajamas, putting together a puzzle. I helped him find his clothes and then went back to the kitchen and put his breakfast on the table. The telephone rang two or three more times and each time Stuart was abrupt while he talked and angry when he hung up. He called Mel Dorn and Gordon Johnson and spoke with them, slowly, seriously, and then he opened a beer and smoked a cigarette while Dean ate, asked him about school, his friends, etc., exactly as if nothing had happened.

Dean wanted to know what he'd done while he was gone, and Stuart took some fish out of the freezer to show him.

"I'm taking him to your mother's for the day," I said.

"Sure," Stuart said and looked at Dean who was holding one of the frozen trout. "If you want to and he wants to, that is. You don't have to, you know. There's nothing wrong."

"I'd like to anyway," I said.

"Can I go swimming there?" Dean asked and wiped his fingers on his pants.

"I believe so," I said. "It's a warm day so take your suit, and I'm sure your grandmother will say it's okay."

Stuart lighted a cigarette and looked at us.

Dean and I drove across town to Stuart's mother's. She lives in an apartment building with a pool and a sauna bath. Her name is Catherine Kane. Her name, Kane, is the same as mine, which seems impossible. Years ago, Stuart has told me, she used to be called Candy by her friends. She is a tall, cold woman with white-blonde hair. She gives me the feeling that she is always judging, judging. I explain briefly in a low voice what has happened (she hasn't yet read the newspaper) and promise to pick Dean up that evening. "He brought his swimming suit," I say. "Stuart and I have to talk about some things," I add vaguely. She looks at me steadily from over her glasses. Then she nods and turns to Dean, saying "How are you, my little man?" She stoops and puts her arms around him. She looks at me again as I open the door to leave. She has a way of looking at me without saying anything.

When I return home Stuart is eating something at the table and drinking beer....

After a time I sweep up the broken dishes and glassware and go outside. Stuart is lying on his back on the grass now, the newspaper and can of beer within reach, staring at the sky. It's breezy but warm out and birds call.

"Stuart, could we go for a drive?" I say. "Anywhere."

He rolls over and looks at me and nods. "We'll pick up some beer," he says. "I hope you're feeling better about this. Try to understand, that's all I ask." He gets to his feet and touches me on the hip as he goes past. "Give me a minute and I'll be ready."

We drive through town without speaking. Before we reach the country he stops at a roadside market for beer. I notice a great stack of papers just inside the door. On the top step a fat woman in a print dress holds out a licorice stick to a little girl. In a few minutes we cross Everson Creek and turn into a picnic area a few feet from the water. The creek flows under the bridge and into a large pond a few hundred yards away. There are a dozen or so men and boys scattered around the banks of the pond under the willows, fishing.

So much water so close to home, why did he have to go miles away to fish?

"Why did you have to go there of all places?" I say.

"The Naches? We always go there. Every year, at least once." We sit on a bench in the sun and he opens two cans of beer and gives one to me. "How the hell was I to know anything like that would happen?" He shakes his head and shrugs, as if it had all happened years ago, or to someone else. "Enjoy the afternoon, Claire. Look at this weather."

"They said they were innocent."

"Who? What are you talking about?"

"The Maddox brothers. They killed a girl named Arlene Hubly near the town where I grew up, and then cut off her head and threw her into the Cle Elum River. She and I went to the same high school. It happened when I was a girl."

"What a hell of a thing to be thinking about," he says. "Come on, get off it. You're going to get me riled in a minute. How about it now? Claire?"

I look at the creek. I float toward the pond, eyes open, face down, staring at the rocks and moss on the creek bottom until I am carried into the lake where I am pushed by the breeze. Nothing will be any different. We will go on and on and on and on. We will go on even now, as if nothing had happened. I look at him across the picnic table with such intensity that his face drains.

"I don't know what's wrong with you," he says. "I don't—"

I slap him before I realize. I raise my hand, wait a fraction of a second, and then slap his cheek hard. This is crazy, I think as I slap him. We need to lock our fingers together. We need to help one another. This is crazy.

He catches my wrist before I can strike again and raises his own hand. I crouch, waiting, and see something come into his eyes and then dart away. He drops his hand. I drift even faster around and around in the pond.

"Come on, get in the car," he says. "I'm taking you home."

"No, no," I say, pulling back from him.

"Come on," he says. "Goddamn it."

"You're not being fair to me," he says later in the car. Fields and trees and farmhouses fly by outside the window. "You're not being fair. To either one of us. Or to Dean, I might add. Think about Dean for a minute. Think about me. Think about someone else besides your goddamn self for a change."

There is nothing I can say to him now. He tries to concentrate on the road, but he keeps looking into the rearview mirror. Out of the corner of his eye, he looks across the seat to where I sit with my knees drawn up under my chin. The sun blazes against my arm and the side of my face. He opens another beer while he drives, drinks from it, then shoves the can between his legs and lets out breath. He knows. I could laugh in his face. I could weep.

2.

Stuart believes he is letting me sleep this morning. But I was awake long before the alarm sounded, thinking, lying on the far side of the bed, away from his hairy legs and his thick, sleeping fingers. He gets Dean off for school, and then he shaves, dresses, and leaves for work. Twice he looks into the bedroom and clears his throat, but I keep my eyes closed.

In the kitchen I find a note from him signed "Love." I sit in the breakfast nook in the sunlight and drink coffee and make a coffee ring on the note. The telephone has stopped ringing, that's something. No more calls since last night. I look at the paper and turn it this way and that on the table. Then I pull it close and read what it says. The body is still unidentified, unclaimed, apparently unmissed. But for the last twenty-four hours men have been examining it, putting things into it, cutting, weighing, measuring, putting back again, sewing up, looking for the exact cause and moment of death. Looking for evidence of rape. I'm sure they hope for rape. Rape would make it easier to understand. The paper says the body will be taken to Keith & Keith Funeral Home pending arrangements. People are asked to come forward with information, etc.

Two things are certain: 1) people no longer care what happens to other people; and 2) nothing makes any real difference any longer. Look at what has happened. Yet nothing will change for

Stuart and me. Really change, I mean. We will grow older, both of us, you can see it in our faces already, in the bathroom mirror, for instance, mornings when we use the bathroom at the same time. And certain things around us will change, become easier or harder, one thing or the other, but nothing will ever really be any different. I believe that. We have made our decisions, our lives have been set in motion, and they will go on and on until they stop. But if that is true, then what? I mean, what if you believe that, but you keep it covered up, until one day something happens that should change something, but then you see nothing is going to change after all. What then? Meanwhile, the people around you continue to talk and act as if you were the same person as yesterday, or last night, or five minutes before, but you are really undergoing a crisis, your heart feels damaged....

The past is unclear. It's as if there is a film over those early years. I can't even be sure that the things I remember happening really happened to me. There was a girl who had a mother and father—the father ran a small cafe where the mother acted as waitress and cashier—who moved as if in a dream through grade school and high school and then, in a year or two, into secretarial school. Later, much later—what happened to the time in between? —she is in another town working as a receptionist for an electronics parts firm and becomes acquainted with one of the engineers who asks her for a date. Eventually, seeing that's his aim, she lets him seduce her. She had an intuition at the time, an insight about the seduction that later, try as she might, she couldn't recall. After a short while they decide to get married, but already the past, her past, is slipping away. The future is something she can't imagine. She smiles, as if she has a secret, when she thinks about the future. Once, during a particularly bad argument, over what she can't now remember, five years or so after they were married, he tells her that someday this affair (his words: "this affair") will end in violence. She remembers this. She files this away somewhere and begins repeating it aloud from time to time. Sometimes she spends the whole morning on her knees in the sandbox behind the garage playing with Dean and one or two of his friends. But every afternoon at four o'clock her head begins to hurt. She holds her forehead and feels dizzy with the pain. Stuart asks her to see a doctor and she does, secretly pleased at the doctor's solicitous attention. She goes away for a while to a place the doctor recommends. Stuart's mother comes out from Ohio in a hurry to care for the child. But she, Claire, spoils everything and returns home in a few weeks. His mother moves out of the house and takes an apartment across town and perches there, as if waiting. One night in bed when they are both near sleep, Claire tells him that she heard some women patients at the clinic discussing fellatio. She thinks this is something he might like to hear. Stuart is pleased at hearing this. He strokes her arm. Things are going to be okay, he says. From now on everything is going to be different and better for them. He has received a promotion and a substantial raise. They've even bought another car, a station wagon, her car. They're going to live in the here and now. He says he feels able to relax for the first time in years. In the dark, he goes on stroking her arm....He continues to bowl and play cards regularly. He goes fishing with three friends of his.

That evening three things happen: Dean says that the children at school told him that his father found a dead body in the river. He wants to know about it.

Stuart explains quickly, leaving out most of the story, saying only that, yes, he and three other men did find a body while they were fishing.

"What kind of body?" Dean asks. "Was it a girl?"

"Yes, it was a girl. A woman. Then we called the sheriff." Stuart looks at me.

"What'd he say?" Dean asks.

"He said he'd take care of it."

"What did it look like? Was it scary?"

"That's enough talk," I say. "Rinse your plate, Dean, and then you're excused."

"But what'd it look like?" he persists. "I want to know."

"You heard me," I say. "Did you hear me, Dean? Dean!" I want to shake him. I want to shake him until he cries.

"Do what your mother says," Stuart tells him quietly. "It was just a body, and that's all there is to it."

I am clearing the table when Stuart comes up behind and touches my arm. His fingers burn. I start, almost losing a plate.

"What's the matter with you?" he says, dropping his hand. "Claire, what is it?"

"You scared me," I say.

"That's what I mean. I should be able to touch you without you jumping out of your skin." He stands in front of me with a little grin, trying to catch my eyes, and then he puts his arm around my waist. With his other hand he takes my free hand and puts it on the front of his pants.

"Please, Stuart." I pull away and he steps back and snaps his fingers.

"Hell with it then," he says. "Be that way if you want. But just remember."

"Remember what?" I say quickly. I look at him and hold my breath.

He shrugs. "Nothing, nothing," he says.

The second thing that happens is that while we are watching television that evening, he in his leather recliner chair, I on the sofa with a blanket and magazine, the house quiet except for the television, a voice cuts into the program to say that the murdered girl has been identified. Full details will follow on the eleven o'clock news.

We look at each other. In a few minutes he gets up and says he is going to fix a nightcap. Do I want one?

"No," I say.

"I don't mind drinking alone," he says. "I thought I'd ask."

I can see he is obscurely hurt, and I look away, ashamed and yet angry at the same time.

He stays in the kitchen a long while, but comes back with his drink just when the news begins.

First the announcer repeats the story of the four local fishermen finding the body. Then the station shows a high school graduation photograph of the girl, a dark-haired girl with a round face and full, smiling lips. There's a film of the girl's parents entering the funeral home to make the identification. Bewildered, sad, they shuffle slowly up the sidewalk to the front steps to where a man in a dark suit stands waiting, holding the door. Then, it seems as if only seconds have passed, as if they have merely gone inside the door and turned around and come out again, the same couple is shown leaving the building, the woman in tears, covering her face with a handkerchief, the man stopping long enough to say to a reporter, "It's her, it's Susan. I can't say anything right now. I hope they get the person or persons who did it before it happens again. This violence...." He motions feebly at the television camera. Then the man and woman get into an old car and drive away into the late afternoon traffic.

The announcer goes on to say that the girl, Susan Miller, had gotten off work as a cashier in a movie theater in Summit, a town 120 miles north of our town. A green, late model car pulled up in front of the theater and the girl, who according to witnesses looked as if she'd been waiting, went over to the car and got in, leading the authorities to suspect that the driver of the car was a friend, or at least an acquaintance. The authorities would like to talk to the driver of the green car.

Stuart clears his throat then leans back in the chair and sips his drink.

The third thing that happens is that after the news Stuart stretches, yawns, and looks at me. I get up and begin making a bed for myself on the sofa.

"What are you doing?" he says, puzzled.

"I'm not sleepy," I say, avoiding his eyes. "I think I'll stay up a while longer and then read something until I fall asleep."

He stares as I spread a sheet over the sofa. When I start to go for a pillow, he stands at the bedroom door, blocking the way.

"I'm going to ask you once more," he says. "What the hell do you think you're going to accomplish by this?"

"I need to be by myself tonight," I say. "I need to have time to think."

He lets out breath. "I'm thinking you're making a big mistake by doing this. I'm thinking you'd better think again about what you're doing. Claire?"

I can't answer. I don't know what I want to say. I turn and begin to tuck in the edges of the blanket. He stares at me a minute longer and then I see him raise his shoulders. "Suit yourself then. I could give a fuck less what you do," he says. He turns and walks down the hall scratching his neck.

*   *   *

This morning I read in the paper that services for Susan Miller are to be held in Chapel of the Pines, Summit, at two o'clock the next afternoon. Also, that police have taken statements from three people who saw her get into the green Chevrolet. But they still have no license number for the car. They are getting warmer, though, and the investigation is continuing. I sit for a long while holding the paper, thinking, then I call to make an appointment at the hairdresser's.

I sit under the dryer with a magazine on my lap and let Millie do my nails.

"I'm going to a funeral tomorrow," I say after we have talked a bit about a girl who no longer works there.

Millie looks up at me and then back at my fingers. "I'm sorry to hear that, Mrs. Kane. I'm real sorry."

"It's a young girl's funeral," I say.

"That's the worst kind. My sister died when I was a girl, and I'm still not over it to this day. Who died?" she says after a minute.

"A girl. We weren't all that close, you know, but still."

"Too bad. I'm real sorry. But we'll get you fixed up for it, don't worry. How's that look?"

"That looks...fine. Millie, did you ever wish you were somebody else, or else just nobody, nothing, nothing at all?"

She looks at me. "I can't say I ever felt that, no. No, if I was somebody else I'd be afraid I might not like who I was." She holds my fingers and seems to think about something for a minute. "I don't know, I just don't know....Let me have your other hand now, Mrs. Kane."

At eleven o'clock that night I make another bed on the sofa and this time Stuart only looks at me, rolls his tongue behind his lips, and goes down the hall to the bedroom. In the night I wake and listen to the wind slamming the gate against the fence. I don't want to be awake, and I lie for a long while with my eyes closed. Finally I get up and go down the hall with my pillow. The light is burning in our bedroom and Stuart is on his back with his mouth open, breathing heavily. I go into Dean's room and get into bed with him. In his sleep he moves over to give me space. I lie there for a minute and then hold him, my face against his hair.

"What is it, mama?" he says.

"Nothing, honey. Go back to sleep. It's nothing, it's all right."

I get up when I hear Stuart's alarm, put on coffee and prepare breakfast while he shaves.

He appears in the kitchen doorway, towel over his bare shoulder, appraising.

"Here's coffee," I say. "Eggs will be ready in a minute."

He nods.

I wake Dean and the three of us have breakfast. Once or twice Stuart looks at me as if he wants to say something, but each time I ask Dean if he wants more milk, more toast, etc.

"I'll call you today," Stuart says as he opens the door.

"I don't think I'll be home today," I say quickly. "I have a lot of things to do today. In fact, I may be late for dinner."

"All right. Sure." He moves his briefcase from one hand to the other. "Maybe we'll go out for dinner tonight? How would you like that?" He keeps looking at me. He's forgotten about the girl already. "Are you all right?"

I move to straighten his tie, then drop my hand. He wants to kiss me goodbye. I move back a step. "Have a nice day then," he says finally. He turns and goes down the walk to his car.

I dress carefully. I try on a hat that I haven't worn in several years and look at myself in the mirror. Then I remove the hat, apply a light makeup, and write a note for Dean.

> *Honey, Mommy has things to do this afternoon, but
> will be home later. You are to stay in the house or in
> the back/yard until one of us comes home.*
>
> *Love*

I look at the word "Love" and then I underline it. As I am writing the note I realize I don't know whether *back yard* is one word or two. I have never considered it before. I think about it and then I draw a line and make two words of it.

I stop for gas and ask directions to Summit. Barry, a forty-year-old mechanic with a moustache, comes out from the restroom and leans against the front fender while the other man, Lewis, puts the hose into the tank and begins to slowly wash the windshield.

"Summit," Barry says, looking at me and smoothing a finger

down each side of his moustache. "There's no best way to get to Summit, Mrs. Kane. It's about a two, two-and-a-half-hour drive each way. Across the mountains. It's quite a drive for a woman. Summit? What's in Summit, Mrs. Kane?"

"I have business," I say, vaguely uneasy. Lewis has gone to wait on another customer.

"Ah. Well, if I wasn't tied up there"—he gestures with his thumb toward the bay—"I'd offer to drive you to Summit and back again. Road's not all that good. I mean it's good enough, there's just a lot of curves and so on."

"I'll be all right. But thank you." He leans against the fender. I can feel his eyes as I open my purse.

Barry takes the credit card. "Don't drive it at night," he says. "It's not all that good a road, like I said. And while I'd be willing to bet you wouldn't have car trouble with this, I know this car, you can never be sure about blowouts and things like that. Just to be on the safe side I'd better check these tires." He taps one of the front tires with his shoe. "We'll run it onto the hoist. Won't take long."

"No, no, it's all right. Really, I can't take any more time. The tires look fine to me."

"Only takes a minute," he says. "Be on the safe side."

"I said no. No! They look fine to me. I have to go now. Barry . . . ."

"Mrs. Kane?"

"I have to go now."

I sign something. He gives me the receipt, the card, some stamps. I put everything into my purse. "You take it easy," he says. "Be seeing you."

As I wait to pull into the traffic, I look back and see him watching. I close my eyes, then open them. He waves.

I turn at the first light, then turn again and drive until I come to the highway and read the sign: SUMMIT 117 Miles. It is ten-thirty and warm.

The highway skirts the edge of town, then passes through farm country, through fields of oats and sugar beets and apple orchards, with here and there a small herd of cattle grazing in open pastures. Then everything changes, the farms become fewer and fewer, more like shacks now than houses, and stands of timber replace the orchards. All at once I'm in the mountains and on the right, far below, I catch glimpses of the Naches River.

In a little while I see a green pickup truck behind me, and it stays behind me for miles. I keep slowing at the wrong times, hoping it will pass, and then increasing my speed, again at the wrong times. I grip the wheel until my fingers hurt. Then on a clear stretch he does pass, but he drives along beside for a minute, a crew-cut man in a blue workshirt in his early thirties, and we look at each other. Then he waves, toots the horn twice, and pulls ahead of me.

I slow down and find a place, a dirt road off of the shoulder. I pull over and turn off the ignition. I can hear the river somewhere down below the trees. Ahead of me the dirt road goes into the trees. Then I hear the pickup returning.

I start the engine just as the truck pulls up behind me. I lock the doors and roll up the windows. Perspiration breaks on my face and arms as I put the car in gear, but there is no place to drive.

"You all right?" the man says as he comes up to the car. "Hello. Hello in there." He raps the glass. "You okay?" He leans his arms on the door and brings his face close to the window.

I stare at him and can't find any words.

"After I passed I slowed up some," he says. "But when I didn't see you in the mirror I pulled off and waited a couple of minutes. When you still didn't show I thought I'd better drive back and check. Is everything all right? How come you're locked up in there?"

I shake my head.

"Come on, roll down your window. Hey, are you sure you're okay? You know it's not good for a woman to be batting around the country by herself." He shakes his head and looks at the highway, then back at me. "Now come on, roll down the window, how about it? We can't talk this way."

"Please, I have to go."

"Open the door, all right?" he says, as if he isn't listening. "At least roll the window down. You're going to smother in there." He looks at my breasts and legs. The skirt has pulled up over my knees. His eyes linger on my legs, but I sit still, afraid to move.

"I want to smother," I say. "I am smothering, can't you see?"

"What in the hell?" he says and moves back from the door. He turns and walks back to his truck. Then, in the side mirror, I watch him returning, and I close my eyes.

"You don't want me to follow you toward Summit or anything? I don't mind. I got some extra time this morning," he says.

I shake my head.

He hesitates and then shrugs. "Okay, lady, have it your way then," he says. "Okay."

I wait until he has reached the highway, and then I back out. He shifts gears and pulls away slowly, looking back at me in his rearview mirror. I stop the car on the shoulder and put my head on the wheel.

The casket is closed and covered with floral sprays. The organ begins soon after I take a seat near the back of the chapel. People begin to file in and find chairs, some middle-aged and older people, but most of them in their early twenties or even younger. They are people who look uncomfortable in their suits and ties, sport coats and slacks, their dark dresses and leather gloves. One boy in flared pants and a yellow short-sleeved shirt takes the chair next to mine and begins to bite his lips. A door opens at one side of the chapel and I look up and for a minute the parking lot reminds me of a meadow. But then the sun flashes on car windows. The family enters in a group and moves into a curtained area off to the side. Chairs creak as they settle themselves. In a few minutes a slim, blond man in a dark suit stands and asks us to bow our heads. He speaks a brief prayer for us, the living, and when he finishes he asks us to pray in silence for the soul of Susan Miller, departed. I close my eyes and remember her picture in the newspaper and on television. I see her leaving the theater and getting into the green Chevrolet. Then I imagine her journey down the river, the nude body hitting rocks, caught at by branches, the body floating and turning, her hair streaming in the water. Then the hands and hair catching in the overhanging branches, holding, until four men come along to stare at her. I can see a man who is drunk (Stuart?) take her by the wrist. Does anyone here know about that? What if these people knew that? I look around at the other faces. There is a connection to be made of these things, these events, these faces, if I can find it. My head aches with the effort to find it.

He talks about Susan Miller's gifts: cheerfulness and beauty, grace and enthusiasm. From behind the closed curtain someone clears his throat, someone else sobs. The organ music begins. The service is over.

Along with the others I file slowly past the casket. Then I move out onto the front steps and into the bright, hot afternoon light. A middle-aged woman who limps as she goes down the stairs ahead of me reaches the sidewalk and looks around, her eyes falling on me. "Well, they got him," she says. "If that's any consolation. They arrested him this morning. I heard it on the radio before I came. A guy right here in town. A longhair, you might have guessed." We move a few steps down the hot sidewalk. People are starting cars. I put out my hand and hold on to a parking meter. Sunlight glances off polished hoods and fenders. My head swims. "He's admitted having relations with her that night, but he says he didn't kill her." She snorts. "They'll put him on probation and then turn him loose."

"He might not have acted alone," I say. "They'll have to be sure. He might be covering up for someone, a brother, or some friends."

"I have known that child since she was a little girl," the woman goes on, and her lips tremble. "She used to come over and I'd bake cookies for her and let her eat them in front of the TV." She looks off and begins shaking her head as the tears roll down her cheeks.

3.

Stuart sits at the table with a drink in front of him. His eyes are red and for a minute I think he has been crying. He looks at me and doesn't say anything. For a wild instant I feel something has happened to Dean, and my heart turns.

"Where is he?" I say. "Where is Dean?"

"Outside," he says.

"Stuart, I'm so afraid, so afraid," I say, leaning against the door.

"What are you afraid of, Claire? Tell me, honey, and maybe I can help. I'd like to help, just try me. That's what husbands are for."

"I can't explain," I say. "I'm just afraid. I feel like, I feel like, I feel like...."

He drains his glass and stands up, not taking his eyes from me. "I think I know what you need, honey. Let me play doctor, okay? Just take it easy now." He reaches an arm around my waist and with his other hand begins to unbutton my jacket, then my blouse. "First things first," he says, trying to joke.

"Not now, please," I say.

"Not now, please," he says, teasing. "Please nothing." Then he steps behind me and locks an arm around my waist. One of his hands slips under my brassiere.

"Stop, stop, stop," I say. I stamp on his toes.

And then I am lifted up and then falling. I sit on the floor looking up at him and my neck hurts and my skirt is over my knees. He leans down and says, "You go to hell then, do you hear, bitch? I hope your cunt drops off before I touch it again." He sobs once and I realize he can't help it, he can't help himself either. I feel a rush of pity for him as he heads for the living room.

He didn't sleep at home last night.

This morning, flowers, red and yellow chrysanthemums. I am drinking coffee when the doorbell rings.

"Mrs. Kane?" the young man says, holding his box of flowers.

I nod and pull the robe tighter at my throat.

"The man who called, he said you'd know." The boy looks at my robe, open at the throat, and touches his cap. He stands with his legs apart, feet firmly planted on the top step. "Have a nice day," he says.

A little later the telephone rings and Stuart says, "Honey, how are you? I'll be home early, I love you. Did you hear me? I love you, I'm sorry, I'll make it up to you. Goodbye, I have to run now."

I put the flowers into a vase in the center of the dining room table and then I move my things into the extra bedroom.

Last night, around midnight, Stuart breaks the lock on my door. He does it just to show me that he can, I suppose, for he doesn't do anything when the door springs open except stand there in his underwear looking surprised and foolish while the anger slips from his face. He shuts the door slowly, and a few minutes later I hear him in the kitchen prying open a tray of ice cubes.

I'm in bed when he calls today to tell me that he's asked his mother to come stay with us for a few days. I wait a minute, thinking about this, and then hang up while he is still talking. But in a little while I dial his number at work. When he finally comes on the line I say, "It doesn't matter, Stuart. Really, I tell you it doesn't matter one way or the other."

"I love you," he says.

He says something else and I listen and nod slowly. I feel sleepy. Then I wake up and say, "For God's sake, Stuart, she was only a child."

THE PARIS REVIEW
INTERVIEW

Raymond Carver lives in a large, two-story, wood-shingled house on a quiet street in Syracuse, New York. The front lawn slopes down to the sidewalk. A new Mercedes sits in the driveway. An older VW, the household car, gets parked on the street.

The entrance to the house is through a large, screened-in porch. Inside, the furnishings are almost without character. Everything matches—cream-colored couches, a glass coffee table. Tess Gallagher, the writer with whom Raymond Carver lives, collects feathers and sets them in vases throughout the house—the most noticeable decorative attempt. My suspicions were confirmed; Carver told me that all the furniture was purchased and delivered in one day.

Gallagher has painted a detachable wood "No Visitors" sign, the lettering surrounded by yellow and orange eyelashes, which hangs on the screen door. Sometimes the phone is unplugged and the sign stays up for days at a time.

Carver works in a large room on the top floor. The surface of the long oak desk is clear; his typewriter is set to the side, on an L-shaped wing. There are no knicknacks, charms or toys of any kind on Carver's desk. He is not a collector or a man prone to mementos and nostalgia. Occasionally, one manila folder lies on the oak desk, containing the story currently in the process of revision. His files are well in order. He can extract a story and all its previous versions at moment's notice. The walls of the study are painted white, like the rest of the house, and like the rest of the house they are mostly bare. Through a high rectangular window above Carver's desk, light filters into the room in slanted beams.

Carver is a large man who wears simple clothes—flannel shirts, khakis or jeans. He seems to live and dress as the characters in his stories live and dress. For someone of his size, he has a remarkably low and indistinct voice, I found myself bending closer every few minutes to catch his words and asking the irritating "What, what?"

Last year, when I visited Syracuse, the "No Visitors" sign was not up and several Syracuse students dropped by to visit during the course of the interview, including Carver's son, a senior. For lunch, Carver made us sandwiches with salmon he had caught off the coast of Washington. Both he and Gallagher are from Washington state and at the time of the interview, they were having a house built in Port Angeles, where they would live part of each year.

This year, the house is completed, and without a phone. Since the time of the interview, Carver has received the Strauss Living Award, given by the Academy of Arts and Letters, and has resigned from his teaching post at Syracuse. For the first time in his life, Carver is a full-time writer.

He once said that the reason he became a short-story writer rather than a novelist was that, in his early life, there was not enough time for the sustained effort of a long work. Now he is starting on a novel.

"It feels different to the extent that I know it's going to be a long haul," Carver said recently in Port Angeles, where he had been in the woods hunting. "I'm anxious to do it. I've never done it before. I want to do a novel more than I want to do anything else. The circumstances of my life all seem to be conjoining at the right time now. I have an idea of the characters. I've been thinking about this material, it's been pulling at me a good long while."

I asked Carver if the house in Washington felt more like a home to him. He replied, "No, wherever I am is fine. This is fine."

INTERVIEWER

What was your early life like, and what made you want to write?

CARVER

I grew up in a small town in eastern Washington, a place called Yakima. My dad worked at the sawmill there. He was a saw-filer and helped take care of the saws that were used to cut and plane the logs. My mother worked as a retail clerk or a waitress or else stayed at home, but she didn't keep any job for very long. I remember talk concerning her "nerves." In the cabinet under the kitchen sink, she kept a bottle of patent "nerve medicine," and she'd take a couple of tablespoons of this every morning. My dad's nerve medicine was whiskey. Most often he kept a bottle of it under the same sink, or else outside in the woodshed. I remember sneaking a taste of it once and hating it, and wondering how anybody could drink the stuff. Home was a little two-bedroom house. We moved a lot when I was a kid, but it was always into another little two-bedroom house. The first house I can remember living in, near the fairgrounds in Yakima, had an outdoor toilet. This was in the late 1940s. I was eight or ten years old then. I used to wait at the bus stop for my dad to come home from work. Usually he was as regular as clockwork. But every two weeks or so, he wouldn't be on the bus. I'd stick around then and wait for the next bus, but I already knew he wasn't going to be on that one, either. When this happened, it meant he'd gone drinking with friends of his from the sawmill. I still remember the sense of doom and hopelessness that hung over the supper table when my mother and I and my kid brother sat down to eat.

INTERVIEWER

But what made you want to write?

CARVER

The only explanation I can give you is that my dad told me lots of stories about himself when he was a kid, and about his dad and his grandfather. His grandfather had fought in the Civil War. He fought for both sides! He was a turncoat. When the South began losing the war, he crossed over to the North and began fighting for the Union forces. My dad laughed when he told this story. He didn't see anything wrong with it, and I guess I didn't either. Anyway, my dad would tell me stories, anecdotes really, no moral to them, about tramping around in the woods, or else riding the rails and having to look out for railroad bulls. I loved his company and loved to listen to him tell me these stories. Once in a while he'd read something to me from what he was reading. Zane Grey westerns. These were the first real hardback books, outside of grade-school texts, and the Bible, that I'd ever seen. It wouldn't happen very often, but now and again I'd see him lying on the bed of an evening and reading from Zane Grey. It seemed a very private act in a house and family that were not given to privacy. I realized that he had this private side to him, something I didn't understand or know anything about, but something that found expression through this occasional reading. I was interested in that side of him and interested in the act itself. I'd ask him to read me what he was reading, and he'd oblige by just reading from wherever he happened to be in the book. After a while he'd say, "Junior, go do something else now." Well, there were plenty of things to do. In those days, I went fishing in this creek that was not too far from our house. A little later, I started hunting ducks and geese and upland game. That's what excited me in those days, hunting and fishing. That's what made a dent in my emotional life, and that's what I wanted to write about.

My reading fare in those days, aside from an occasional historical novel or Mickey Spillane mystery, consisted of *Sports Afield* and *Outdoor Life*, and *Field and Stream*. I wrote a longish thing about the fish that got away, or the fish I caught, one or the other, and asked my mother if she would type it up for me. She couldn't type, but she did go rent a typewriter, bless her heart, and between the two of us, we typed it up in some terrible fashion and sent it out. I remember there were two addresses on the masthead of the outdoors magazine; so we sent it to the office closest to us, to Boulder, Colorado, the circulation department. The piece came back, finally, but that was fine. It had gone out in the world, that manuscript—it had been places. Somebody had read it besides my mother, or so I hoped anyway. Then I saw an ad in *Writer's Digest*. It was a photograph of a man, a successful author, obviously, testifying to something called the Palmer Institute of Authorship. That seemed like just the thing for me. There was a monthly payment plan involved. Twenty dollars down, ten or fifteen dollars a month for three years or thirty years, one of those things. There were weekly assignments with personal responses to the assignments. I stayed with it for a few months. Then, maybe I got bored, I stopped doing the work. My folks stopped making the payments. Pretty soon a letter arrived from the Palmer Institute telling me that if I paid them up in full, I could still get the certificate of completion. This seemed more than fair. Somehow I talked my folks into paying the rest of the money, and in due time I got the certificate and hung it up on my bedroom wall. But all through high school it was assumed that I'd graduate and go to work at the sawmill. For a long time I wanted to do the kind of work my dad did. He was going to ask his foreman at the mill to put me on after I graduated. So I worked at the mill for about six months. But I hated the work and knew from the first day I didn't want to do that for the rest of my life. I worked long enough to save the money for a car, buy some clothes, and so I could move out and get married.

INTERVIEWER

Somehow, for whatever reasons, you went to college. Was it your wife who wanted you to go on to college? Did she encourage you in this respect? Did she want to go to college and that made you want to go? How old were you at this point? She must have been pretty young, too.

CARVER

I was eighteen. She was sixteen and pregnant and had just graduated from an Episcopalian private school for girls in Walla Walla, Washington. At school she'd learned the right way to hold a teacup; she'd had religious instruction and gym and such, but she also learned about physics and literature and foreign languages. I was terrifically impressed that she knew Latin. Latin! She tried off and on to go to college during those first years, but it was too hard to do that; it was impossible to do that and raise a family and be broke all the time, too. I mean broke. Her family didn't have any money. She was going to that school on a scholarship. Her mother hated me and still does. My wife was supposed to graduate and go to the University of Washington to study law on a fellowship. Instead, I made her pregnant, and we got married and began our life together. She was seventeen when the first child was born, eighteen when the second was born. What shall I say at this point? We didn't have any youth. We found ourselves in roles we didn't know how to play. But we did the best we could. Better than that I want to think. She did finish college finally. She got her B.A. degree at San Jose State twelve or fourteen years after we married.

INTERVIEWER

Were you writing during these early, difficult years?

CARVER

I worked nights and went to school days. We were always working. She was working and trying to raise the kids and manage a household. She worked for the telephone company. The kids were with a babysitter during the day. Finally, I graduated with the B.A. degree from Chico State College and we put everything into the car and in one of those carry-alls that fits on top of your car, and we went to Iowa City. A teacher named Dick Day at Humboldt State had told me about the Iowa Writers' Workshop. Day had sent along a story of mine and three or four poems to Don Justice who was responsible for getting me a five hundred dollar grant at Iowa.

INTERVIEWER

Five hundred dollars?

CARVER

That's all they had, they said. It seemed like a lot at the

time. But I didn't finish at Iowa. They offered me more money to stay on the second year, but we just couldn't do it. I was working in the library for a dollar or two an hour, and my wife was working as a waitress. It was going to take me another year to get a degree, and we just couldn't stick it out. So we moved back to California. This time it was Sacramento. I found work as a night janitor at Mercy Hospital. I kept the job for three years. It was a pretty good job. I only had to work two or three hours a night, but I was paid for eight hours. There was a certain amount of work that had to get done, but once it was done, that was it—I could go home or do anything I wanted. The first year or two I went home every night and would be in bed at a reasonable hour and be able to get up in the morning and write. The kids would be off at the babysitter's and my wife would have gone to her job—a door-to-door sales job. I'd have all day in front of me. This was fine for a while. Then I began getting off work at night and going drinking instead of going home. By this time it was 1967 or 1968.

INTERVIEWER

When did you first get published?

CARVER

When I was an undergraduate at Humboldt State in Arcata, California. One day, I had a short story taken at one magazine and a poem taken at another. It was a terrific day! Maybe one of the best days ever. My wife and I drove around town and showed the letters of acceptance to all of our friends. It gave some much-needed validation to our lives.

INTERVIEWER

What was the first story you ever published? And the first poem?

CARVER

It was a story called "Pastoral" and it was published in the *Western Humanities Review*. It's a good literary magazine and it's still being published by the University of Utah. They didn't pay me anything for the story, but that didn't matter. The poem was called "The Brass Ring," and it was published by a magazine in Arizona, now defunct, called *Targets*. Charles Bukowski had a poem in the same issue, and I was pleased to be in the same magazine with him. He was a kind of hero to me then.

INTERVIEWER

Is it true—a friend of yours told me this—that you celebrated your first publication by taking the magazine to bed with you?

CARVER

That's partly true. Actually, it was a book, *The Best American Short Stories* annual. My story "Will You Please Be Quiet, Please?" had just appeared in the collection. That was back in the late sixties when it was edited every year by Martha Foley and people used to call it that—simply, "The Foley Collection." The story had been published in an obscure little magazine out of Chicago called *December*. The day the anthology came in the mail I took it to bed to read and just to look at, you know, and hold it, but I did more looking and holding than actual reading. I fell asleep and woke up the next morning with the book there in bed beside me, along with my wife.

INTERVIEWER

In an article you did for the *New York Times Book Review* you mentioned a story "too tedious to talk about here"—about why you choose to write short stories over novels. Do you want to go into that story now?

CARVER

The story that was "too tedious to talk about" has to do with a number of things that aren't very pleasant to talk about. I did finally talk about some of these things in the essay "Fires," which was published in *Antaeus*. In it I said that finally, a writer is judged by what he writes, and that's the way it should be. The circumstances surrounding the writing are something else, something extra-literary. Nobody ever asked me to be a writer. But it *was* tough to stay alive and pay bills and put food on the table and at the same time to think of myself as a writer and to *learn* to write. After years of working crap jobs and raising kids and trying to write, I realized I needed to write things I could finish and be done with in a hurry. There was no way I could undertake a novel, a two or three year stretch of work on a single project. I needed to write something I could get some kind of a payoff from immediately, not next year, or three years from now. Hence, poems and stories. I was beginning to see that my life was not—let's say it was not what I wanted it to be. There was always a wagonload of frustration to deal with—wanting to write and not being able to find the time or the place for it. I used to go out and sit in the car and try to write something on a pad on my knee. This was when the kids were in their adolescence. I was in my late twenties or early thirties. We were still in a state of penury, we had one bankruptcy behind us, and years of hard work with nothing to show for it except an old car, a rented house and new creditors on our backs. It was depressing, and I felt spiritually obliterated. Alcohol became a problem. I more or less gave up, threw in the towel, and took to full-time drinking as a serious pursuit. That's part of what I was talking about when I was talking about things "too tedious to talk about."

INTERVIEWER

Could you talk a little more about the drinking? So many writers, even if they're not alcoholics, drink so much.

CARVER

Probably not a whole lot more than any other group of professionals. You'd be surprised. Of course there's a mythology that goes along with the drinking, but I was never into that. I was into the drinking itself. I suppose I began to drink heavily after I'd realized that the things I'd wanted most in life for myself and my writing, and my wife and children, were simply not going to happen. It's strange. You never start out in life with the intention of becoming a bankrupt or an alcoholic or a cheat and a thief. Or a liar.

INTERVIEWER

And you were all those things?

CARVER

I was. I'm not any longer. Oh, I lie a little from time to time, like everyone else.

INTERVIEWER

How long since you quit drinking?

CARVER

June second, 1977. If you want the truth, I'm prouder of that, that I've quit drinking, than I am of anything in my life. I'm a recovered alcoholic. I'll always be an alcoholic, but I'm no longer a practicing alcoholic.

INTERVIEWER

How bad did the drinking get?

CARVER

It's very painful to think about some of the things that happened back then. I made a wasteland out of everything I touched. But I might add that towards the end of the drinking there wasn't much left anyway. But specific things? Let's just say, on occasion, the police were involved and emergency rooms and courtrooms.

INTERVIEWER

How did you stop? What made you able to stop?

CARVER

The last year of my drinking, 1977, I was in a recovery center twice, as well as one hospital; and I spent a few days in a place called DeWitt near San Jose, California. DeWitt used to be, appropriately enough, a hospital for the criminally insane.

Toward the end of my drinking career I was completely out of control and in a very grave place. Blackouts, the whole business—points where you can't remember anything you say or do during a certain period of time. You might drive a car, give a reading, teach a class, set a broken leg, go to bed with someone, and not have any memory of it later. You're on some kind of automatic pilot. I have an image of myself sitting in my living room with a glass of whiskey in my hand and my head bandaged from a fall caused by an alcoholic seizure. Crazy! Two weeks later I was back in a recovery center, this time at a place called Duffy's, in Calistoga, California, up in the wine country. I was at Duffy's on two different occasions; in the place called DeWitt, in San Jose; and in a hospital in San Francisco—all in the space of twelve months. I guess that's pretty bad. I was dying from it, plain and simple, and I'm not exaggerating.

INTERVIEWER

What brought you to the point where you could stop drinking for good?

CARVER

It was late May 1977. I was living by myself in a house in a little town in northern California, and I'd been sober for about three weeks. I drove to San Francisco where they were having this publishers' convention. Fred Hills, at that time editor-in-chief at McGraw-Hill, wanted to take me to lunch and offer me money to write a novel. But a couple of nights before the lunch, one of my friends had a party. Midway through, I picked up a glass of wine and drank it, and that's the last thing I remember. Blackout time. The next morning when the stores opened, I was waiting to buy a bottle. The dinner that night was a disaster; it was terrible, people quarreling and disappearing from the table. And the next morning I had to get up and go have this lunch with Fred Hills. I was so hung over when I woke up I could hardly hold my head up. But I drank a half pint of vodka before I picked up Hills and that helped, for the short run. And then he wanted to drive over to Sausalito for lunch! That took us at least an hour in heavy traffic, and I was drunk and hung over both, you understand. But for some reason he went ahead and offered me this money to write a novel.

INTERVIEWER

Did you ever write the novel?

CARVER

Not yet! Anyway, I managed to get out of San Francisco back up to where I lived. I stayed drunk for a couple more days. And then I woke up, feeling terrible, but I didn't drink anything that morning. Nothing alcoholic, I mean. I felt terrible physically—mentally, too, of course—but I didn't drink anything. I didn't drink for three days, and when the third day had passed, I began to feel some better. Then I just kept not drinking. Gradually I began to put a little distance between myself and the booze. A week. Two weeks. Suddenly it was a month. I'd been sober for a month, and I was slowly starting to get well.

INTERVIEWER

Did AA help?

CARVER

It helped a lot. I went to at least one and sometimes two meetings a day for the first month.

INTERVIEWER

Did you ever feel that alcohol was in any way an inspiration? I'm thinking of your poem "Vodka," published in *Esquire*.

CARVER

My God, no! I hope I've made that clear. Cheever remarked that he could always recognize "an alcoholic line" in a writer's work. I'm not exactly sure what he meant by this but I think I know. When we were teaching in the Iowa Writers' Workshop in the fall semester of 1973, he and I did nothing *but* drink. I mean we met our classes, in a manner of speaking. But the entire time we were there—we were living in this hotel they have on campus, the Iowa House—I don't think either of us ever took the covers off our typewriters. We made trips to a liquor store twice a week in my car.

INTERVIEWER

To stock up?

CARVER

Yes, stock up. But the store didn't open until ten A.M. Once we planned an early morning run, a ten o'clock run and we were going to meet in the lobby of the hotel. I came down early to get some cigarettes and John was pacing up and down in the lobby. He was wearing loafers, but he didn't have any socks on. Anyway, we headed out a little early. By the time we got to the liquor store the clerk was just unlocking the front door. On this particular morning, John got out of the car before I could get it properly parked. By the time I got inside the store he was already at the checkout stand with a half gallon of Scotch. He lived on the fourth floor of the hotel and I lived on the second. Our rooms were identical, right down to the same reproduction of the same painting hanging on the wall. But when we drank together, we always drank in his room. He said he was afraid to come down to drink on the second floor. He said there was always a chance of him getting mugged in the hallway! But you know, of course, that fortunately, not too long after Cheever left Iowa City, he went to a treatment center and got sober and stayed sober until he died.

INTERVIEWER

Do you feel the spoken confessions at Alcoholics Anonymous meetings have influenced your writing?

CARVER

There are different kinds of meetings—speaker meetings where just one speaker will get up and talk for fifty minutes or so about what it was like then, and maybe what it's like now.

And there are meetings where everyone in the room has a chance to say something. But I can't honestly say I've ever consciously or otherwise patterned any of my stories on things I've heard at the meetings.

INTERVIEWER

Where do your stories come from, then? I'm especially asking about the stories that have something to do with drinking.

CARVER

The fiction I'm most interested in has lines of reference to the real world. None of my stories really *happened*, of course. But there's always something, some element, something said to me or that I witnessed, that may be the starting place. Here's an example: "That's the last Christmas you'll ever ruin for us!" I was drunk when I heard that, but I remembered it. And later, much later, when I was sober, using only that one line and other things I imagined, imagined so accurately that they *could* have happened, I made a story—"A Serious Talk."

But the fiction I'm most interested in, whether it's Tolstoy's fiction, Chekhov, Barry Hannah, Richard Ford, Hemingway, Isaac Babel, Ann Beattie or Anne Tyler, strikes me as autobiographical to some extent. At the very least it's referential. Stories long or short don't just come out of thin air. I'm reminded of a conversation involving John Cheever. We were sitting around a table in Iowa City with some people and he happened to remark that after a family fracas at his home one night, he got up the next morning and went into the bathroom to find something his daughter had written in lipstick on the bathroom mirror: "D-e-r-e daddy, don't leave us." Someone at the table spoke up and said, "I recognize that from one of your stories." Cheever said, "Probably so. Everything I write is autobiographical." Now of course that's not literally true. But everything we write is, in some way, autobiographical. I'm not in the least bothered by "autobiographical" fiction. To the contrary. *On The Road*. Céline. Roth. Lawrence Durrell in *The Alexandria Quartet*. So much of Hemingway in the Nick Adams stories. Updike, too, you bet, Jim McConkey. Clark

Blaise is a contemporary writer whose fiction is out-and-out autobiography. Of course, you have to know what you're doing when you turn your life's stories into fiction. You have to be immensely daring, very skilled and imaginative and willing to tell everything on yourself. You're told time and again when you're young to write about what you know, and what do you know better than your own secrets? But unless you're a special kind of writer, and a very talented one, it's dangerous to try and write volume after volume on the Story of My Life. A great danger, or at least a great temptation, for many writers is to become too autobiographical in their approach to their fiction. A little autobiography and a lot of imagination are best.

INTERVIEWER

Are your characters trying to do what matters?

CARVER

I think they are trying. But trying and succeeding are two different matters. In some lives, people always succeed; and I think it's grand when that happens. In other lives, people don't succeed at what they try to do, at the things they want most to do, the large or small things that support the life. These lives are, of course, valid to write about, the lives of the people who don't succeed. Most of my own experience, direct or indirect, has to do with the latter situation. I think most of my characters would like their actions to count for something. But at the same time they've reached the point—as so many people do—that they know it isn't so. It doesn't add up any longer. The things you once thought important or even worth dying for aren't worth a nickel now. It's their lives they've become uncomfortable with, lives they see breaking down. They'd like to set things right, but they can't. And usually they do know it, I think, and after that they just do the best they can.

INTERVIEWER

Could you say something about one of my favorite stories in

What We Talk About? Where did the idea for "Why Don't You Dance?" originate?

CARVER

I was visiting some writer friends in Missoula back in the mid-1970s. We were all sitting around drinking and someone told a story about a barmaid named Linda who got drunk with her boyfriend one night and decided to move all of her bedroom furnishings into the backyard. They did it, too, right down to the carpet and the bedroom lamp, the bed, the nightstand, everything. There were about four or five writers in the room, and after the guy finished telling the story, someone said, "Well, who's going to write it?" I don't know who else might have written it, but I wrote it. Not then, but later. About four or five years later, I think. I changed and added things to it, of course. Actually, it was the first story I wrote after I finally stopped drinking.

INTERVIEWER

What are your writing habits like? Are you always working on a story?

CARVER

When I'm writing, I write every day. It's lovely when that's happening. One day dovetailing into the next. Sometimes I don't even know what day of the week it is. The "paddlewheel of days" John Ashbery has called it. When I'm not writing, like now, when I'm tied up with teaching duties as I have been the last while, it's as if I've never written a word or had any desire to write. I fall into bad habits. I stay up too late and sleep in too long. But it's okay. I've learned to be patient and to bide my time. I had to learn that a long time ago. Patience. If I believed in signs, I suppose my sign would be the sign of the turtle. I write in fits and starts. But when I'm writing, I put in a lot of hours at the desk, ten or twelve of fifteen hours at a stretch, day after day. I love that, when that's happening. Much of this work time, understand, is given over to revising and rewriting. There's not much that I like better than to take a story that

I've had around the house for a while and work it over again. It's the same with the poems I write. I'm in no hurry to send something off just after I write it, and I sometimes keep it around the house for months doing this or that to it, taking this out and putting that in. It doesn't take that long to do the first draft of the story, that usually happens in one sitting, but it does take a while to do the various versions of the story. I've done as many as twenty or thirty drafts of a story. Never less than ten or twelve drafts. It's instructive, and heartening both, to look at the early drafts of great writers. I'm thinking of the photographs of galleys belonging to Tolstoy, to name one writer who loved to revise. I mean, I don't know if he loved it or not, but he did a great deal of it. He was always revising, right down to the time of page proofs. He went through and rewrote *War and Peace* eight times and was still making corrections in the galleys. Things like this should hearten every writer whose first drafts are dreadful, like mine are.

INTERVIEWER

Describe what happens when you write a story.

CARVER

I write the first draft quickly, as I said. This is most often done in longhand. I simply fill up the pages as rapidly as I can. In some cases, there's a kind of personal shorthand, notes to myself for what I will do later when I come back to it. Some scenes I have to leave unfinished, unwritten in some cases; the scenes that will require meticulous care later. I mean all of it requires meticulous care—but some scenes I save until the second or third draft, because to do them and do them right would take too much time on the first draft. With the first draft it's a question of getting down the outline, the scaffolding of the story. Then on subsequent revisons I'll see to the rest of it. When I've finished the longhand draft I'll type a version of the story and go from there. It always looks different to me, better, of course, after it's typed up. When I'm typing the first draft, I'll begin to rewrite and add and delete a little then. The real work comes later, after I've done three or four drafts of the story. It's the same with the poems, only the poems may go through forty or fifty drafts. Donald Hall told me he sometimes writes a hundred or so drafts of his poems. Can you imagine?

INTERVIEWER

Has your way of working changed?

CARVER

The stories in *What We Talk About* are different to an extent. For one thing, it's a much more self-conscious book in the sense of how intentional every move was, how calculated. I pushed and pulled and worked with those stories before they went into the book to an extent I'd never done with any other stories. When the book was put together and in the hands of my publisher, I didn't write anything at all for six months. And then the first story I wrote was "Cathedral," which I feel is totally different in conception and execution from any stories that have come before. I suppose it reflects a change in my life as much as it does in my way of writing. When I wrote "Cathedral" I experienced this rush and I felt, "This is what it's all about, this is the reason we do this." It was different than the stories that had come before. There was an opening up when I wrote the story. I knew I'd gone as far the other way as I could or wanted to go, cutting everything down to the marrow, not just to the bone. Any farther in that direction and I'd be at a dead end—writing stuff and publishing stuff I wouldn't want to read myself, and that's the truth. In a review of the last book, somebody called me a "minimalist" writer. The reviewer meant it as a compliment. But I didn't like it. There's something about "minimalist" that smacks of smallness of vision and execution that I don't like. But all of the stories in the new book, the one called *Cathedral*, were written within an eighteen-month period; and in every one of them I feel this difference.

INTERVIEWER

Do you have any sense of an audience? Updike described his

ideal reader as a young boy in a small midwestern town finding one of his books on a library shelf.

CARVER

It's nice to think of Updike's idealized reader. But except for the early stories, I don't think it's a young boy in a small midwestern town who's reading Updike. What would this young boy make of *The Centaur* or *Couples* or *Rabbit Redux* or *The Coup*? I think Updike is writing for the audience that John Cheever said he was writing for, "intelligent, adult men and women," wherever they live. Any writer worth his salt writes as well and as truly as he can and hopes for as large and perceptive a readership as possible. So you write as well as you can and hope for good readers. But I think you're also writing for other writers to an extent—the dead writers whose work you admire, as well as the living writers you like to read If they like it, the other writers, there's a good chance other "intelligent, adult men and women" may like it, too. But I don't have that boy you mentioned, or anyone else in mind for that matter, when I'm doing the writing itself.

INTERVIEWER

How much of what you write do you finally throw away?

CARVER

Lots. If the first draft of the stjory is forty pages long, it'll usually be half that by the time I'm finished with it. And it's not just a question of taking out or bringing it down. I take out a lot, but I also add things and then add some more and take out some more. It's something I love to do, putting words in and taking words out.

INTERVIEWER

Has the process of revision changed now that the stories seem to be longer and more generous?

CARVER

Generous, yes, that's a good word for them. Yes, and I'll tell you why. Up at school there's a typist who has one of those space-age typewriters, a word processor, and I can give her a story to type and once she has it typed and I get back the fair copy, I can mark it up to my heart's content and give it back to her; and the next day I can have my story back, all fair copy once more. Then I can mark it up again as much as I want, and the next day I'll have back a fair copy once more. I love it. It may seem like a small thing, really, but it's changed my life, that woman and her word processor.

INTERVIEWER

Did you ever have any time off from having to earn a living?

CARVER

I had a year once. It was a very important year for me, too. I wrote most of the stories in *Will You Please Be Quiet, Please?* in that year. It was back in 1970 or 1971. I was working for this textbook publishing firm in Palo Alto. It was my first white collar job, right after the period when I'd been a janitor at the hospital in Sacramento. I'd been working away there quietly as an editor when the company, it was called SRA, decided to do a major reorganization. I planned to quit, I was writing my letter of resignation, but then suddenly—I was fired. It was just wonderful the way it turned out. We invited all of our friends that weekend and had a firing party! For a year I didn't have to work. I drew unemployment and had my severance pay to live on. And that's the period when my wife finished her college degree. That was a turning point, that time. It was a good period.

INTERVIEWER

Are you religious?

CARVER

No, but I have to believe in miracles and the possibility of resurrection. No question about that. Every day that I wake up, I'm glad to wake up. That's why I like to wake up early. In my drinking days I would sleep until noon or whatever and I would usually wake up with the shakes.

INTERVIEWER

Do you regret a lot of things that happened back then when things were so bad?

CARVER

I can't change anything now. I can't afford to regret. That life is simply gone now, and I can't regret its passing. I have to live in the present. The life back then is gone just as surely—it's as remote to me as if it had happened to somebody I read about in a nineteenth-century novel. I don't spend more than five minutes a month in the past. The past really *is* a foreign country, and they do do things differently there. Things happen. I really do feel I've had two different lives.

INTERVIEWER

Can you talk a little about literary influences, or at least name some writers whose work you greatly admire?

CARVER

Ernest Hemingway is one. The early stories. "Big Two-Hearted River," "Cat in the Rain," "The Three-Day Blow," "Soldier's Home," lots more. Chekhov. I suppose he's the writer whose work I most admire. But who doesn't like Chekhov? I'm talking about his stories now, not the plays. His plays move too slowly for me. Tolstoy. Any of his short stories, novellas, and *Anna Karenina*. Not *War and Peace*. Too slow. But *The Death of Ivan Ilyich, Master and Man*, "How Much Land Does A Man Need?" Tolstoy is the best there is. Isaac Babel, Flannery O'Connor, Frank O'Connor. James Joyce's *Dubliners*. John Cheever. *Madame Bovary*. Last year I reread that book, along with a new translation of Flaubert's letters written while he was composing—no other word for it— *Madame Bovary*. Conrad. Updike's *Too Far To Go*. And there are wonderful writers I've come across in the last year or two like Tobias Wolff. His book of stories *In the Garden of the North American Martyrs* is just wonderful. Max Schott. Joy Williams. Bobbie Ann Mason. Did I mention her? Well, she's good and worth mentioning twice. Harold Pinter. V.S. Prichett. Years ago I read something in a letter by Chekhov that impressed me. It was a piece of advice to one of his many correspondents, and it went something like this: Friend, you don't have to write about extraordinary people who accomplish extraordinary and memorable deeds. (Understand I was in college at the time and reading plays about princes and dukes and the overthrow of kingdoms. Quests and the like, large undertakings to establish heroes in their rightful places. Novels with larger-than-life heroes.) But reading what Chekhov had to say in that letter, and in other letters of his as well, and reading his stories, made me see things differently than I had before. Not long afterwards I read a play and a number of stories by Maxim Gorky, and he simply reinforced in his work what Chekhov had to say. Richard Ford is another fine writer. He's primarily a novelist, but he's also written stories and essays. He's a friend. I have a lot of friends who are good friends, and some of them are good writers. Some not so good.

INTERVIEWER

What do you do in that case? I mean, how do you handle that—if one of your friends publishes something you don't like?

CARVER

I don't say anything unless the friend asks me, and I hope he doesn't. But if you're asked you have to say what you think, of course. But you try to say it in a way that it doesn't wreck the friendship. You want your friends to do well and write the best they can. But sometimes their work is a disappointment. You want everything to go well for them, but you have this dread that maybe it won't and there's not much you can do.

INTERVIEWER

What do you think of moral fiction? I guess this has to lead into talk about John Gardner and his influence on you. I know you were his student many years ago at Chico State College.

CARVER

That's true. I've written about our relationship in the *Antaeus* piece and elaborated on it more in my introduction to a posthumous book of his called *On Becoming a Novelist*. I think *On Moral Fiction* is a wonderfully smart book. I don't agree with all of it, by any means, but generally he's right. Not so much in his assessments of living writers as in the aims, the aspirations of the book. It's a book that wants to affirm life rather than trash it. Gardner's definition of morality is life-affirming. And in that regard he believes good fiction is moral fiction. It's a book to argue with, if you like to argue. It's brilliant, in any case. I think he may argue his case even better in *On Becoming a Novelist*. And he doesn't go after other writers as he did in *On Moral Fiction*. We had been out of touch with each other for years when he published *On Moral Fiction*, but his influence, the things he stood for in my life when I was his student, were still so strong that for a long while I didn't want to read the book. I was afraid to find out that what I'd been writing all these years was immoral! You understand that we'd not seen each other for nearly twenty years and had only renewed our friendship after I'd moved to Syracuse and he was down there at Binghamton, seventy miles away. There was a lot of anger directed toward Gardner and the book when it was published. He touched nerves. I happen to think it's a remarkable piece of work.

INTERVIEWER

But after you read the book, what did you think then about your own work? Were you writing "moral" or "immoral" stories?

CARVER

I'm still not sure! But I heard from other people, and then he told me himself, that he liked my work. Especially the new work. That pleases me a great deal. Read *On Becoming a Novelist*.

INTERVIEWER

Do you still write poetry?

CARVER

Some, but not enough. I want to write more. If too long a period of time goes by, six months or so, I get nervous if I haven't written any poems. I find myself wondering if I've stopped being a poet or stopped being able to write poetry. It's usually then that I sit down and try to write some poems. This book of mine, *Fires*—that's got all of the poems I want to keep.

INTERVIEWER

How do they influence each other? The writing of fiction and the writing of poetry?

CARVER

They don't any longer. For a long time I was equally interested in the writing of poetry and the writing of fiction. In magazines I always turned to the poems first before I read the stories. Finally, I had to make a choice, and I came down on the side of the fiction. It was the right choice for me. I'm not a "born" poet. I don't know if I'm a "born" anything except a white American male. Maybe I'll become an occasional poet. But I'll settle for that. That's better than not being any kind of poet at all.

INTERVIEWER

How has fame changed you?

CARVER

I feel uncomfortable with that word. You see, I started out with such low expectations in the first place—I mean how far are you going to get in this life writing short stories? And I didn't have much self-esteem as a result of this drinking thing. So it's a continual amazement to me, this attention that's come along. But I can tell you that after the reception for *What We Talk About*, I felt a confidence that I've never felt before. Every good thing that's happened since has conjoined to make me want to do even more and better work. It's been a good spur. And all this coming at a time in my life when I have more strength than I've ever had before. Do you know what I'm saying? I feel stronger and more certain of my direction now than ever before. So "fame"—or let's say this new-found attention and interest—has been a good thing. It bolstered my confidence, when my confidence needed bolstering.

INTERVIEWER

Who reads your writing first?

CARVER

Tess Gallagher. As you know, she's a poet and short-story writer herself. I show her everything I write except for letters, and I've even shown her a few of those. But she has a wonderful eye and a way of feeling herself into what I write. I don't show her anything until I've marked it up and taken it as far as I can. That's usually the fourth or fifth draft, and then she reads every subsequent draft thereafter. So far I've dedicated three books to her and those dedications are not just a token of love and affection; they also indicate the high esteem in which I hold her and an acknowledgement of the help and inspiration she's given me.

INTERVIEWER

Where does Gordon Lish enter into this? I know he's your editor at Knopf.

CARVER

Just as he was the editor who began publishing my stories at *Esquire* back in the early 1970s. But we had a friendship that went back before that time, back to 1967 or 1968, in Palo Alto. He was working for a textbook publishing firm right across the street from the firm where I worked. The one that fired me. He didn't keep any regular office hours. He did most of his work for the company at home. At least once a week he'd ask me over to his place for lunch. He wouldn't eat anything himself, he'd just cook something for me and then hover around the table watching me eat. It made me nervous, as you might imagine. I'd always wind up leaving something on my plate, and he'd always wind up eating it. Said it had to do with the way he was brought up. This is not an isolated example. He still does things like that. He'll take me to lunch now and won't order anything for himself except a drink and then he'll eat up whatever I leave in my plate! I saw him do it once in the Russian Tea Room. There were four of us for dinner, and after the food came he watched us eat. When he saw we were going to leave food on our plates, he cleaned it right up. Aside from this craziness, which is more funny than anything, he's remarkably smart and sensitive to the needs of a manuscript. He's a good editor. Maybe he's a great editor. All I know for sure is that he's my editor and my friend, and I'm glad on both counts.

INTERVIEWER

Would you consider doing more movie script work?

CARVER

If the subject could be as interesting as this one I just finished with Michael Cimino on the life of Dostoyevsky, yes, of course. Otherwise, no. But Dostoyevsky! You bet I would.

INTERVIEWER

And there was real money involved.

CARVER

Yes.

INTERVIEWER

That accounts for the Mercedes.

CARVER

That's it.

INTERVIEWER

What about the *New Yorker?* Did you ever send your stories to the *New Yorker* when you were first starting out?

CARVER

No, I didn't. I didn't read the *New Yorker.* I sent my stories and poems to the little magazines and once in a while something was accepted, and I was made happy by the acceptance. I had some kind of audience, you see, even though I never met any of my audience.

INTERVIEWER

Do you get letters from people who've read your work?

CARVER

Letters, tapes, sometimes photographs. Somebody just sent me a cassette—songs that had been made out of some of the stories.

INTERVIEWER

Do you write better on the West Coast—out in Washington—or here in the East? I guess I'm asking how important a sense of place is to your work.

CARVER

Once, it was important to see myself as a writer from a particular place. It was important for me to be a writer from the West. But that's not true any longer, for better or worse. I think I've moved around too much, lived in too many places, felt dislocated and displaced, to now have any firmly-rooted sense of "place." If I've ever gone about consciously locating a story in a particular place and period, and I guess I have, especially in the first book, I suppose that place would be the Pacific Northwest. I admire the sense of place in such writers as Jim Welch, Wallace Stegner, John Keeble, William Eastlake, and William Kittredge. There are plenty of good writers with this sense of place you're talking about. But the majority of my stories are not set in any specific locale. I mean they could take place in just about any city or urban area; here in Syracuse, but also Tucson, Sacramento, San Jose, San Francisco, Seattle, or Port Angeles, Washington. In any case, most of my stories are set indoors!

INTERVIEWER

Do you work in a particular place in your house?

CARVER

Yes, upstairs in my study. It's important to me to have my own place. Lots of days go by when we just unplug the telephone and put out our "No Visitors" sign. For many years I worked at the kitchen table, or in a library carrel, or else out in my car. This room of my own is a luxury *and* a necessity now.

INTERVIEWER

Do you still hunt and fish?

CARVER

Not so much any more. I still fish a little, fish for salmon in the summer, if I'm out in Washington. But I don't hunt, I'm sorry to say. I don't know where to go! I guess I could find someone who'd take me, but I just haven't gotten around to it. But my friend Richard Ford is a hunter. When he was up here in the spring of 1981 to give a reading from his work, he took the proceeds from his reading and bought me a shotgun. Imagine that! And he had it inscribed, "For Raymond from Richard, April 1981." Richard is a hunter you see, and I think he was trying to encourage me.

INTERVIEWER

How do you hope your stories will affect people? Do you think your writing will change anybody?

CARVER

I really don't know. I doubt it. Not change in any profound sense. Maybe not any change at all. After all, art is a form of entertainment, yes? For both the maker and the consumer. I mean in a way it's like shooting billiards or playing cards, or bowling—it's just a different, and I would say higher, form of amusement. I'm not saying there isn't spiritual nourishment involved, too. There is, of course. Listening to a Beethoven concerto or spending time in front of a Van Gogh painting or reading a poem by Blake can be a profound experience on a scale that playing bridge or bowling a '220' game can never be. Art is all the things art is supposed to be. But art is also a superior amusement. Am I wrong in thinking this? I don't know. But I remember in my twenties reading plays by Strindberg, a novel by Max Frisch, Rilke's poetry, listening all night to music by Bartok, watching a TV special on the Sistine Chapel and Michaelangelo and feeling in each case that my life *had* to change after these experiences, it couldn't help but be affected by these experiences and *changed*. There was simply no way I would not become a different person. But then I found out soon enough my life was not going to change after all. Not in any way that I could see, perceptible or otherwise. I understood then that art was something I could pursue when I had the time for it, when I could afford to do so, and that's all. Art was a luxury and it wasn't going to change me or my life. I guess I came to the hard realization that art doesn't make anything happen. No. I don't believe for a minute in that absurd Shellyian nonsense having to do with poets as the "unacknowledged legislators" of this world. What an idea! Isak Dinesen said that she wrote a little every day, without hope and without despair. I like that. The days are gone, if they were ever with us, when a novel or a play or a book of poems could change people's ideas about the world they live in or even about themselves. Maybe writing fiction about particular kinds of people living particular kinds of lives will allow certain areas of life to be understood a little better than they were understood before. But I'm afraid that's it, at least as far as I'm concerned. Perhaps it's different in poetry. Tess has had letters from people who have read her poems and say the poems saved them from jumping off a cliff or drowning themselves, etc. But that's something else. Good fiction is partly a bringing of the news from one world to another. That end is good in and of itself, I think. But changing things through fiction, changing somebody's political affiliation or the political system itself, or saving the whales or the redwood trees, no. Not if these are the kinds of changes you mean. And I don't think it should have to do any of these things, either. It doesn't *have* to do anything. It just has to be there for the fierce pleasure we take in doing it, and the different kind of pleasure that's taken in reading something that's durable and made to last, as well as beautiful in and of itself. Something that throws off these sparks—a persistent and steady glow, however dim.

MONA SIMPSON & LEWIS BUZBEE
Summer 1983

AFTERWORD

When I was asked if I'd like to write a Foreword to this book, I said I didn't think so. But the more I thought on it, it seemed to me a few words might be in order. But not a Foreword, I said. Somehow a Foreword seemed presumptuous. Forewords and Prefaces to one's own work, in fiction or poetry, ought to be reserved for literary eminences over the age of fifty, say. But maybe, I said, an Afterword. So what follows then, for better or worse, are a few words after the fact.

The poems I've chosen to include were written between 1966 and 1982. Some of them first appeared in book form in *Near Klamath*, *Winter Insomnia*, and *At Night the Salmon Move*. I've also included poems that were written since the publication, in 1976, of *At Night the Salmon Move*—poems which have appeared in magazines and journals but not yet in a book. The poems have not been put into a chronological order. Instead, they have been more or less arranged into broad groups having to do with a particular way of thinking and feeling about things—a constellation of feelings and attitudes—that I found at work when I began looking at the poems with an eye toward collecting them for this book. Some of the poems seemed to fall naturally into certain areas, or obsessions. There were, for instance, a number of them that had to do in one way or another with alcohol; some with foreign travel and personages; others strictly concerned with things domestic and familiar. So this became the ordering principle when I went to arrange the book. For example, in 1972 I wrote and published a poem called "Cheers." Ten years later, in 1982, in a vastly different life and after many poems of a different nature entirely, I found myself writing and publishing a poem called "Alcohol." So when the time came to make a selection of poems for this book, it was the content, or obsession (I don't care for the word "theme") which most often suggested where the

217

poems would go. Nothing particularly noteworthy or remarkable about this process.

One final word: in nearly every instance the poems that appeared in the earlier books have been slightly, in some cases ever so slightly, revised. But they have been revised. They were revised this summer, and I think they've been made better in the process. But more about revision later.

The two essays were written in 1981, and I was asked to write them. In one case, an editor at the *New York Times Book Review* wanted me to write on "any aspect of writing" and the little piece "On Writing" was the result. The other came about through an invitation to contribute something to a book on "influences" called *In Praise of What Persists* which was being put together by Steve Berg of *American Poetry Review*, and Ted Solotaroff at Harper and Row. My contribution was "Fires"—and it was Noel Young's idea that we call this book after that title.

The earliest story, "The Cabin," was written in 1966, was collected in *Furious Seasons*, and was revised this summer for publication here. *Indiana Review* will publish the story in their Fall 1982 number. A much more recent story is "The Pheasant," which will be published this month in a limited edition series by Metacom Press and will appear later this fall in *New England Review*.

I like to mess around with my stories. I'd rather tinker with a story after writing it, and then tinker some more, changing this, changing that, than have to write the story in the first place. That initial writing just seems to me the hard place I have to get to in order to go on and have fun with the story. Rewriting for me is not a chore—it's something I like to do. I think by nature I'm more deliberate and careful than I am spontaneous, and maybe that explains something. Maybe not. Maybe there's no connection except the one I'm making. But I do know that revising the work once it's done is something that comes naturally to me and is something I take pleasure in doing. Maybe I revise because it gradually takes me into the heart of what the story is *about*. I have to keep trying to see if I can find that out. It's a process more than a fixed position.

There was a time when I used to think it was a character defect that made me have to struggle along like this. I don't think this way any longer. Frank O'Connor has said that he was always revising his stories (this after sometimes taking the story through twenty or thirty rewrites in the first place) and that someday he'd like to publish a revised book of his revisions. To a limited extent, I've had that opportunity here. Two of the stories, "Distance" and "So Much Water So Close to Home" (from the original eight stories that made up *Furious Seasons*), were first published in book form in FS and were then included in *What We Talk About When We Talk About Love*. When Capra approached me about reprinting, between two covers, *Furious Seasons* and *At Night the Salmon Move*—both books were then out of print—the idea of this book began to take hold. But I was in something of a quandary about these two particular stories Capra wanted to include. They had both been largely rewritten for the Knopf book. After some deliberation, I decided to stay fairly close to the versions as they first appeared in the Capra Press book, but this time hold the revisions to a minimum. They *have* been revised again, but not nearly so much as they once were. But how long can this go on? I mean, I suppose there is, finally, a law of diminishing returns. But I can say now that I prefer the later versions of the stories, which is more in accord with the way I am writing short stories these days.

So all of the stories here have been reworked, to a greater or lesser degree; and they are somewhat different now than the original versions published either in magazines or in *Furious Seasons*. I see this as an instance in which I am in the happy position of being able to make the stories better than they were. At least, God knows, I *hope* they're better. I think so anyway. But, truly, I've seldom seen a piece of prose, or a poem—my own or anyone else's—that couldn't be improved upon if it were left alone for a time.

I'm grateful to Noel Young for giving me the opportunity, and the initiative, to look at the work once more and see what could be done with it.

RAYMOND CARVER
Syracuse, New York
September 7, 1982

ABOUT THE AUTHOR

Raymond Carver was born in 1939. He was a Guggenheim Fellow in 1979 and has twice been awarded grants by the National Endowment for the Arts. He has taught at the University of Iowa, the University of Texas, and the University of California, and in 1983 he resigned his chair at Syracuse University in order to accept a much-coveted Mildred and Harold Strauss Living award. In addition to his books of short fiction, he has brought out three collections of poetry. His work has been widely anthologized, and he was the 1983 first-place winner in William Abrahams's distinguished short-fiction annual, *Prize Stories: The O. Henry Awards.* Mr. Carver now lives in the Pacific Northwest.